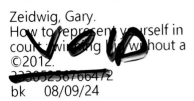

How to Represent Yourself in Court

Winning Big without a Lawyer

Gary Zeidwig
Attorney at Law

How to Represent Yourself in Court
Copyright © Gary Zeidwig 2012

Book and Cover Design by Perseus Design

Visit us on the Web at www.BGPublishingInternational.com

Published by BG Publishing International
1304 SW 160th Avenue, Suite 203, Sunrise FL 33326

ISBN-13: 978-0-936977-00-3
ISBN-10: 0936977000

With pride and love, I dedicate this book to my father, Howard M. Zeidwig, who was the perfect dad and role model. When I was a boy, I couldn't wait to be an attorney, not because I knew anything about the law, but because my father was an attorney and I wanted to be just like him. One of Broward County's best trial attorneys, he taught me to always fight for the truth and believe in my clients.

TABLE OF CONTENTS

INTRODUCTION

THE BASICS

Many people today elect to represent themselves in their legal proceedings. This book is designed to help those of you wishing to represent yourself in court to navigate the process as successfully as possible, and understand the advantages and potential disadvantages of self-representation.

Representing Yourself is your guide to competently prepare yourself from start to finish when bringing or defending against a court case and serves as your compass when navigating the often confusing route through the court system. It will familiarize you with the numerous important legal terms you will encounter, and prepare you academically as well as mentally for the challenges you will face, should you find yourself in such a circumstance.

It is important to note that *Representing Yourself* focuses primarily on proceedings within the State Court system. Although you may have occasion to bring a case in Federal Court, it is far likelier that you will find yourself in one of America's State Courts. Throughout, *Representing Yourself* stresses the importance of doing your homework carefully and comprehensively to improve your chances of success when representing yourself.

The first step is to understand the differences that exist between criminal and civil matters, and determine in which court your case will be heard. This is important for several reasons, not the least of which is to verify the precise time frame in which you have to make your claim. Every claim has an established time frame or limit, referred to as the Statute of Limitations, which will vary based upon the type of claim you have and the State in which your claim will be adjudicated. *Representing Yourself* will familiarize you with the typical courthouse layout, including who is typically found inside and how the courthouse itself is set up. You will learn about the established official Rules of Court, which apply to both the courthouse and the courtroom and to which you must adhere at all times. Key tips on proper court etiquette are also furnished so you can proceed more comfortably and confidently, something that is particularly critical when presenting your case before a jury.

In addition, when you represent yourself, it is very important to build and maintain what is referred to as a Trial Notebook, your comprehensive, portable file of all your pertinent research, preparation materials and all documents filed with the court concerning your case. *Representing Yourself* will instruct you step by step how to construct this trial notebook most effectively and what types of documents are critical to include, so that you always have them at your fingertips. This trial notebook will be your constant loyal companion from inception through your preparation phase, the penultimate pretrial stage and on through the ultimate trial.

You will be taken through each and every pretrial stage, commencing from the time you file your initial claim all the way through to the eve of the trial. This book will explain precisely what information must be contained in both the initial Complaint and the corresponding Answer, and what the consequences will be if you fail to follow through correctly on either of these.

The section covering pretrial discovery is where you will learn what pretrial motions may be made, and how to raise objections during the discovery process; also what is involved in Court-Ordered Mediation and what makes up the Pretrial Order, the court-ordered guide for every single participant in your particular trial.

Following the pretrial section, you will be led through the opening of a typical trial right through to its end and how to appeal an adverse ruling. You will learn how juries work and how to make them work for you. You will learn how to question witnesses — yours and those of your adversary — as well as any possible experts participating in the proceedings. You will learn what constitutes evidence and how to get it admitted, and review various motions that can and possibly should be made before, during, and after your trial. You will learn how and why to make objections and how the court handles them. Techniques to help you create an effective Opening Statement and Closing Argument to the jury are also covered. Additionally, pointers on how to best to present yourself to the court and jury in order to make the most positive impact are listed for easy reference.

With your trial notebook and these techniques and recommendations in hand, you should be ready for virtually anything that comes about during your court proceeding. Where applicable, case studies have been inserted. Please note: in order to protect the privacy of specific clients, the case studies represented herein are composite case studies. Actual names and identifying information have been altered, and comparable incidents of multiple clients have been combined into one case study for the purposes of this book.

CHAPTER
1

TERMINOLOGY

It is helpful to have some basic terminology at your fingertips in the event you decide to bring a case on your own. All the terms contained in this book that appear in boldface may be found along with their definitions in the glossary at the end of this book, however, here are some of the commonly encountered legal terms and their relationships to each other.

The **Plaintiff** is the person or persons, also known as the *party* or *litigant* who initiates a lawsuit. The lawsuit is filed because the Plaintiff believes a case, or **Cause of Action,** exists against the **Defendant.** The Plaintiff is, therefore, said to **Sue** the Defendant if the Cause of Action is actually filed with the Court. The Plaintiff may bring witnesses and present **Evidence,** such as documents and photographs to prove the Plaintiff's case.

The Defendant is the person or persons being sued, the party against whom the Plaintiff's case is brought. If the case is being heard in Court versus having reached a settlement prior to a trial, this means the Defendant denies all or part of the case being brought by the Plaintiff, and is exercising the right to present witnesses and Evidence to disprove the Plaintiff's claims.

The **Court** is another name for the **Judge**, who makes each and every decision on all issues regarding Evidence, determining what can and cannot be shown (made admissible) to the **Jury**, if there is one. The Court/Judge may decide the case alone, based upon all the admissible (permitted) Evidence, without benefit of a Jury. A non-Jury trial such as this is often called a **Judge Trial** or **Bench Trial**.

A Jury comprises either six or twelve people, called **Jurors**, who are asked to decide a case either unanimously or by majority rule. For each Jury, there are typically one or two additional **Alternates** chosen in the event a Juror is dismissed or unable to continue service during the trial. The Alternate sits through the entire trial alongside the jury, however, if no Juror replacement was made during the trial, the Alternate does not retire with the Jury to the jury room to deliberate when the case is over.

Civil versus Criminal

A criminal case results when a criminal law has been broken. When this occurs, then it is said to be the State's or the People's interests at stake and the object is to punish the guilty party by means of fines, imprisonment, or, in extreme cases, death where permissible.

In a criminal matter, the Defendant is always entitled to a jury trial, and has the right to an appointed attorney at the government's expense. Unfortunately, there is no such right in civil cases, although in the Federal Court System one can ask for an appointed attorney based on financial hardship. There are also organizations that can provide you with an attorney for specific types of actions, either free of charge or at a reduced rate. This varies from state to state. Check with your local bar association or the Clerk's Office for information regarding what organizations may be available in your area.

In a civil case, the matter generally boils down to money, such as when a contract is broken or someone is involved in an automobile accident. There are times, however, when other remedies are sought in a civil case, such as a change of child custody. (The remedies afforded by equitable jurisdiction of the Courts are discussed in Chapter Five.)

The right to a jury trial in civil cases depends upon the case and State in which the case has been filed. Generally, there is a right to jury trial in negligence matters: automobile accidents, medical malpractice, etc. No such right in cases such as child custody exists. Whether you are entitled to fully twelve jurors or fewer depends upon the case that is being tried and the jurisdiction in which it is located. In Florida, for example, Florida Statute §69.071 provides that, in all civil cases, a jury of six shall be sufficient. Georgia, by contrast, as recently as 1995, allowed juries of twelve in civil actions. Times have changed, however and, in Georgia, it now depends upon the amount in controversy.[1] Six-person juries are even becoming more prevalent in criminal cases, so do not expect to automatically get a jury of twelve should you decide to represent yourself.[2]

In criminal matters, the case against the Defendant must be proved beyond a **Reasonable Doubt.** The term "reasonable doubt," contrary to what popular culture would like us to believe, is not the same thing as "beyond a shadow of a doubt." Instead, it consists of some nebulous, lesser amount of doubt that jurors must puzzle out based on the Court's instructions at the end of each case, before deliberations begin. In civil cases, the jury must decide the case based on a **Preponderance of the Evidence**. Again, the Court will define for the jury what constitutes a preponderance of evidence at the end of the case.

Regardless, if you are the Defendant in this particular matter, this does not prevent you from reminding the jury, both in your **Opening Statement** and your **Closing Argument**, that the Plaintiff bears this **Burden of Proof** and while making those statements you can reinforce just what that burden of proof entails.

A more comprehensive list of legal terms may be found in the glossary beginning on page 93.

---

[1] Baker, Frank. *Judicial Information.* 27 Aug. 2010. Cobb County State Court Administration. 1 Feb. 2011. http://www.cobbcountyga.gov/judicial/#statecourtclerk.
[2] Holmquist, Jill P. *Does Jury Size Still Matter?* An Open Question. Mar. 2010. The Jury Expert: The Art and Science of Litigation. 27 Aug. 2010. http://www.astcweb.org/public/publication/article.cfm/1/22/3/Does-Jury-Size-Still-Matter.

CHAPTER
2

YOU CAN BE YOUR OWN LAWYER

Pro Se

If you handle your own lawsuit, you are said to be proceeding **Pro Se**. In its simplest terms, Pro Se means, "without a lawyer." You may wonder: *who would even attempt to represent themselves instead of retaining a lawyer?* You may be surprised to learn that many people do, and do so successfully. Pro Se statistics from Family Court in the Ninth Judicial Circuit of Florida reveal a steady increase in the percentages of Pro Se litigants between 1999 and 2001 from an already high 66 percent to 73 percent.[1]

According to statistics collected by the Utah State Courts, 49 percent of petitioners (Plaintiffs) and 81 percent of respondents (Defendants) in divorce cases choose to represent themselves. These figures increase to 99 percent of both petitioners and respondents in small claims cases.

New Hampshire reports that 85 percent of all litigants (both Plaintiffs and Defendants) with civil cases in the District Court, and 48

---

[1] Herman, Madelynn. *Knowledge and Information Services; Self Representation; Pro Se Statistics; Memorandum.* 25 Sept. 2006. National Center for State Courts. Feb. 2011. http://www.ncsonline.org/WC/Publications/Memos/ProSeStatsMemo.htm#statecourt.

percent of all those in the Superior Court, elect not to be represented by attorneys. In family law matters, 70 percent of litigants in Superior Court are Pro Se, while at least one party chooses to proceed without representation in 97 percent of domestic violence cases in District Court.

These are statistics from just a few courts in three of the fifty United States. You can just imagine how this translates to the number of people nationwide who elect to represent themselves in the many U.S. courts each year.

Why Be Your Own Lawyer?

According to a study conducted by the National Center for State Courts, the number of people who choose to represent themselves rather than seek help by hiring a lawyer is increasing, because those people believe that:

1.   Lawyers are too expensive
2.   Courts and lawyers do not deliver quality services
3.   Their cases are simple enough to handle themselves

Civil Court analysts give the following additional reasons for the increase in Pro Se litigants:

1.   People want greater control over their cases
2.   Lawyers often lack a good "bedside manner," inadequately explaining to clients what is happening with their cases
3.   Many people distrust lawyers, due to negative personal experiences and negative images of lawyers portrayed on TV and in books, movies, and the media in general
4.   Legal assistance is available from other sources, including but not limited to the Internet, computer software, and paralegal or other legal document providers

Proceeding Pro Se

If you think that to represent yourself is beyond your capabilities, let me assure you that it is not. The most important thing to

10

remember is not to throw your common sense out the window. When determining the pertinent facts in your case, your common sense and life experience can and should guide you. You are intelligent. You are capable of asking intelligent, observant, penetrating questions. You are capable of determining what evidence and which witnesses people will and will not believe. These are important tools to put together a good, effective case on your own behalf. The pivotal point for success is time — you must put in the time and put in sufficient time. You will need plenty of it. If a lawyer is representing the other side, then the time and effort you expend beforehand is particularly critical. Contrary to popular belief or what popular culture tells us, much of what goes on in a lawsuit happens *before the trial ever begins*. In fact, it's possible and even likely that most of your case can be handled (organized) before you even file suit, assuming that you are not in danger of missing your **Statute of Limitations** deadline.

If you are willing to put in the time and are not afraid to roll up your sleeves and shoulder some hard work, you have what it takes to represent yourself. There are times, however, when you should never proceed alone; times when you absolutely need a professional. Cases that involve complex legal issues, cases where the liability (fault) is not clear or simply proved, and cases involving the termination of parental rights, as well as most criminal cases, fall under the umbrella of when you require the services of an experienced lawyer.

When Should You Be Your Own Lawyer?

Contract cases or automobile accident cases where the issue of who is at fault is either not being argued or is fairly straightforward are instances in which you can safely go it alone. More difficult cases may also fall within your capability as long as you are willing to invest sufficient time and effort.

For the most part, straightforward cases deal in straightforward facts; however, it is still important to familiarize yourself with the laws that apply to your case. Law libraries are open to everyone. Often the law librarian on staff can assist you in finding what you need; even a lawyer who is conducting his or her own research might be willing to point you in the right direction. This will be discussed in more detail in Chapter Five, however, you should know that you may likely need to spend some time at your local law library prior to trial in order to research cases that support your own and possibly dispute the grounds that your opposing litigant is putting forth. It is unquestionably time well spent.

Besides possessing a willingness to spend time preparing for your case, you also must be willing to recognize when you are in over your head and ask for help. Even the seemingly simplest case can turn into a hydra-headed monster. One consideration is to hire an attorney on a piecemeal basis — that is, go to the attorney only on those occasions, for example, when you need a complicated document created or if you need help with your legal research. Although in the past, lawyers have been reluctant to give such piecemeal representation, this "unbundling" is becoming more common.

In addition, many States now allow paralegals to provide document services, and there is much help available on the Web. Check your State's laws regarding paralegal assistance, if that is something you would like to consider. It is important to note that paralegals are *not* trained attorneys, and, although they can prepare documents for you in some cases, they cannot give you legal advice. As for the Web, you just have to be patient and sift through the myriad sites and sources.

Preparing Yourself

If you want to be respected, to be taken seriously, you need to take yourself and the proceedings seriously. The way you look affects how you feel. Equally, or even more important, the way you look affects how others respond to you. If you go into Court wearing ratty jeans and a T-shirt boasting an amusing slogan, the jury is going to think you are just as casual about your case. If you go in dressed nicely, whether that means a suit, a button-down or polo shirt, a businesslike dress or skirt, the jury is going to view you differently. The same will be true in a judge/bench trial, where there is no jury.

It is frequently said, "Clothes make the man." Well, they can also make the case. Let me give you an example. When I practiced in Northwest Florida, I had a system. For jury selection (we'll discuss this in greater depth later on), I deliberately chose a neutral-looking outfit: neutral design and neutral colors. I was meeting the jurors for the first time and first impressions are important. I did not want anything strong to influence their opinions of me, consciously or subconsciously. Usually, we would have jury selection, Opening Statements, and maybe one or two witnesses on the first day. After that, I would develop a feel for the jury's temperament. I would choose my next suit based on that assessment: color, style, everything.

On the last day of the trial when it was time for me to make my Closing Statement, when I felt very assured of my case and my client, I would choose a suit that was professional but considerably more stylish, with a stronger dash of color. I did this for two reasons: one, I wanted the jury to know that I felt good, that I had confidence in myself, my case and my client; and two, I wanted their eyes on me and me alone — I wanted their undivided attention. I am a big believer in the end game. Everything you do during the trial should lead up to your closing argument.

If you are going to invest considerable time and effort to handle your case competently and efficiently by yourself, you must make that same effort to look professional and responsible. You need to look like you care about your case and that you take it very, very seriously.

Dealing with the other party

1. When dealing with the other party (litigant), always be honest about all the facts. Anything less will always come back to bite you.
2. Be cooperative. This does not mean you have to give away the farm, but simply that it should not feel frustrating to deal with you.
3. Never deal directly with the other party if they have a lawyer; always deal exclusively with their lawyer. No exceptions.
4. Answer all letters and phone calls. Judges do not look kindly upon uncooperative litigants, Pro Se or otherwise. Not only do you risk angering the judge, but it also makes for a miserable

working relationship. Show the other party the respect you expect in return.

CHAPTER
3

THE COURT AND ITS RULES

The State Court System

Each State has its own hierarchy of Courts. Every State has Courts of limited jurisdiction and Courts of general jurisdiction, as well as Appeals Courts. In one State, the lower Court may be referred to as the Municipal Court; in another State it may be called the Small Claims Court.

The Trial Courts of general jurisdiction typically cover only certain types of cases and/or have an established threshold amount that you must meet in order for the Court to take jurisdiction of your case. These Courts may be called anything from Circuit to District to Superior Courts.

Florida's Small Claims Court, for example, handles claims up to and including $5,000. You pay nominal filing fees and Court costs to cover the expense of serving both the Complaint (lawsuit) and the Summons to Answer on your Defendant(s). At the time of this writing, the filing fees run anywhere from $55 to about $400, and the service fees range from the cost of a certified mailer to having the sheriff go out and hand deliver your Complaint and Summons at a rate of $10 per Defendant. If your Defendant lives outside the County, you may have to contact the County sheriff in that jurisdiction to make arrangements and pay for the service of your Complaint and Summons.

Generally, you will find the Small Claims Court to be the most user-friendly arena when it comes to getting you started, by providing you with forms and assistance along the way. However, although the clerks and their staff can help you fill out forms, *they cannot give you any legal advice,* and this includes any advice about your particular case. Ask for a copy of the Small Claims Court rules. They will indicate, among other things, which rules of the higher Court do not apply to the Small Claims Court.

To continue this example, in Florida cases with a value of over $5,000 up to and including $15,000, the County Court has jurisdiction. The County Court also hears cases such as misdemeanor criminal matters, traffic (ticket-related) cases, and evictions.

If your case involves a matter of controversy in excess of $15,000, or if it involves a felony or a matter of **Equitable Jurisdiction**, it falls under the domain of the Circuit Court. Equitable Jurisdiction involves the filing of an injunction (asking the Court to stop someone from doing something); the filing of a **Declaratory Judgment** (asking the Court to declare that a specific position is the correct one); or asking for **Specific Performance** (asking that the Court require a person or company to do a thing they previously promised to do but to date have not).

As in the Small Claims Court, you can receive some assistance in the County and Circuit Courts. For example, Florida Statute §28.215 provides that the Circuit Court Clerks shall provide ministerial services to Pro Se litigants, but, again, they are never permitted to dispense legal advice.

Once you determine what Court is appropriate for your case, you must pay a fee to file your case there. Every Court (and every State) differs in their fee schedules. If you cannot afford to pay the Court costs, there may be programs that allow you to file an affidavit of poverty. (See, for example, Florida's O.C.G.A§ 9-15-2.) Your Court costs would then be waived in whole or in part, depending upon your situation.

This does not, however, insulate you from a possible attorney's fee award later in the case. For instance, if you bring a case against someone and you lose the case, depending on the nature of the case, the Court may award attorney's fees against you. This means that you have to pay the other party's attorney's fees. If your case is judged to have been brought in bad faith, then attorney's fees will most assuredly be awarded against you.

Similar to Small Claims Court, Circuit Court costs range anywhere from a few dollars to several hundred dollars, depending on the Court and the case you have brought. Florida Statute §28.241(1)(a), for example, governs what filing fees can be charged in civil cases in their Circuit Courts according to case type. Pursuant to that statute, most civil actions filed in the Circuit Court would cost you up to $399 to file if you had fewer than five Defendants. As with the Small Claims Court, this does not include the service fees for hand delivery of the Summons to Defendant (s) or certified mailing costs, whichever the Court deems appropriate.

What happens if you file in the wrong Court?

Let us say that you initially file in Small Claims Court, believing that your claim is worth $5,000 or less. Now let us say that the first time the Court (Judge) looks at your case, the Judge realizes that it is worth much more. Therefore, because it does not meet the jurisdictional requirements of this particular Court, the Judge simply transfers it to the County Court where the jurisdictional requirements are $15,000 or less.

You may also find yourself needing to **Appeal** a lower Court's decision, which means that you are asking a higher Court to review the outcome of the lower Court with the hope that the ruling may be overturned. In Florida, the County Courts, including Small Claims Courts, appeal directly to the Circuit Courts. Circuit Court cases are appealable directly to the District Court of Appeal, which, in turn, takes its Appeals directly to the Supreme Court of Florida. Cases from the Circuit Court can also be directly appealed to the Supreme Court of Florida, depending on the case. The District Court of Appeals can take Appeals from County Court cases where questions have been **certified** to that Court. The same is true, among other methods, for getting to the Supreme Court of Florida from the District Court of Appeal. Take some time early on to determine the system in your home State, in the event you find yourself needing to use it. You need to know how to maneuver from one Court to the other and determine how much it is going to cost. The County Clerk's Office should be able to assist you. (See below.)

The Courthouse

Most Courthouses are comparable in how they are set up and operate. They contain the offices of the Clerk, the District (State) Attorney, the Public Defender (if your County has one), Property Records, Tag, and the Judge, plus the law library, Traffic Court and the other Courtrooms. Other offices may be housed here as well. The Clerk's office may be divided into County and Circuit Court Clerks, and have separate divisions for civil, criminal and sometimes domestic relations.

The Clerk's Office

This is one of the most important offices in the Courthouse, as far as you are concerned. Here, you will file all your case paperwork and the Clerk will keep a running record of every piece of paper that is filed in your case *by all parties.* This is important to remember, because if you lose your copy, or if you are not sure whether you have been copied with something, the original will always be found in the Clerk's file.

The Clerk's Office is also a good place to obtain information, including on the Courthouse, the Courtrooms, and Court procedures, and even help you fill out forms. Again, what they cannot and must not do is give you legal advice. Because of that mandate, you may find some Court clerks and their employees to be a little aloof toward Pro Se parties. Still, the Clerk's office is an excellent place to start when you are trying to find your way around the Court.

The Courtroom

If you are bringing a case, it's very helpful to familiarize yourself with the layout of the Courtroom beforehand. If you have a jury trial,

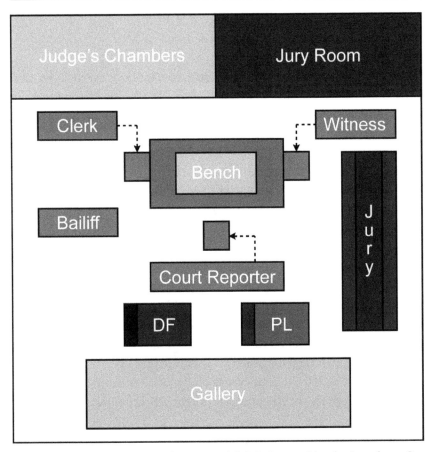

the Plaintiff sits closest to the jury, which is located in the jury box. So, if you are the Plaintiff bringing the lawsuit, you will sit at the table next to the jury box. The Judge is usually sitting up on a platform looking down on the court. This is referred to as being "on the Bench."

To the right of the Judge you typically find his **Court Clerk** and/or the **Bailiff**. The clerk keeps the Judge's calendar, often referred to as the docket. A bailiff is usually assigned to each Courtroom and, when you enter, you will inform either the clerk or the bailiff that you are present and ready to be heard. The clerk controls the exhibits during the trial and either the clerk or the **Court Reporter** administers oaths to the witnesses and interpreters. The Judge frequently administers the oaths to the jurors.

The **Court Reporter** is often seated in front of the bench. A Court reporter transcribes the entire proceedings of a motion, deposition, hearing, or the trial.

The jury room is where the jury goes to deliberate on their verdict.

The gallery is where the spectators sit. Most trials are open to the public and you may want to avail yourself of this and watch a trial or two to get a feel for how things work.

Courtroom Rules and Etiquette

Good manners are essential. You must always be polite and respectful to the judge, all parties, and witnesses. Address people with appropriate titles such as Mr., Mrs., Ms., Dr., etc., along with their last names. Never address someone by their first name, even if you know them, as this may come across as your being overly familiar, rude or condescending. Professionalism is paramount.

When addressing or being addressed by the Judge, always refer to the Judge as "Your Honor." *NEVER* argue with a judge's ruling. It does not do you any good, and the Judge has the power to impose sanctions (punishments) against you, depending upon how offensive your behavior is. Plus, if your case is being heard in front of a jury, this reflects very poorly on you and can potentially influence the outcome of your case.

At this point, the various etiquette referred to will make reference to particular situations in which you will find yourself in the Courtroom during the trial. All these procedures will be discussed in greater detail further on. This is merely to imbue you with a sense of decorum and procedure.

Whenever you give a document to the Court, you must first share a copy with opposing counsel. There is never an exception to this rule. For example, say you are presenting a Memorandum to the Court during the proceedings. You take two copies of your Memorandum out of your Trial Notebook and give one to opposing counsel, and then politely request to approach the Bench. When permission is granted, you approach in what is called a **Sidebar** and hand your Memo to the Court (either the Judge or the Judge's clerk, depending on your Court's protocol).

When it comes to proffering Evidence, you will have already shown it to the other party's counsel (attorney) at the **Pretrial Conference.** However, if you intend to use it for any purpose during the trial, always make the showing of walking to counsel table with your pre-marked exhibit, even if counsel waives you away each time.

Never speak directly to opposing counsel during the trial. It is permissible when showing documents to identify what you are showing before giving them to the Court, but conversations between counsel are forbidden.

Rules of Court

Not to be confused with generally accepted Court etiquette, the official Rules of Court are published and usually bound in a softback book that you can view at the Court's law library. They are also available for purchase, a wise investment. Your County Clerk should be able to advise you where you can purchase a copy.

The Rules of Court contain the rules of procedure for the various Courts in a given County or Circuit. (A Circuit consists of several Counties that fall under the same set of rules and judges, and they follow the same law.) There may be many Circuits in a State, all following versions of the law. Conversely, sometimes a separate book will exist for each Court. Again, invest in a copy that applies to the Court that will adjudicate your case. Not only do they contain the procedural Rules of Court, but, more important, they contain the deadlines that apply for performing all actions in that Court, including filing documents, pretrial actions and trial proceedings. They are very strict and if you miss one, you are out of luck. The last thing you want is to be judged to have admitted to something you haven't done simply because you failed to answer on time. The Local Rules will advise you how the judges in that County or Circuit want things handled, inside their Courtrooms and out.

Timing Is Everything

"Am I filing this in time?" This is first and foremost what you must keep in mind before you bring your lawsuit. This comes even before worrying about whether you have sufficient Evidence. Every jurisdiction has a **Statute of Limitations** and that Statute of Limitations varies. Not only does it vary with each State, but also with regard to the lawsuit as well. So if it has been a few years since your incident happened, since your **Cause of Action** "accrued," you need to determine before anything else what your time limit is in which to get your lawsuit filed. This is because, although you will want to set aside time to negotiate a settlement of the matter with the other party first, if you have only a few days left in which to file, you must file your lawsuit first, before any negotiations, in advance of that deadline. There are no extensions. If you fail to file before the court-established deadline, you will likely forfeit your right to bring your lawsuit altogether. So, before you start compiling your case or even negotiating a settlement, always ensure first that you are well inside the deadline to file your case.

For example, in Florida, the Statute of Limitations for an automobile accident is four years; medical malpractice actions must be brought within two years. Some States have Statutes of Limitations as short as one year. Understand that the Statute of Limitations is jurisdictional, which means that if you fail to bring your lawsuit within the time prescribed, the Court is not able to exercise jurisdiction over the cause of action. It has no power or authority over the case. Extensions are not allowed. If you snooze, you lose. Delay does not pay.

CHAPTER

4

THE FRAMEWORK OF A LAWSUIT

Not all lawsuits are the same, but most follow a similar path. Examples are provided here for your understanding, however, greater detail will be provided in Chapter Five.

A Wrong Occurs

Perhaps a contract is breached, or a car wreck occurs, or someone fails to pay child support — this is a crucial, legal element of your claim. If you do not have a legally addressable wrong, then you cannot bring a suit. For instance, say someone did something terrible to you that upset you deeply. Although there is arguably a cause of action for the "Intentional Infliction of Emotional Distress," the standard for such cases is extremely high. Or, say, you get one of those mailers that states that you have won a trip to Hawaii or a particular sweepstake with pages and pages of confusing and hard to understand fine print. One Florida attorney had an elderly lady come in with one of those and even *he* thought she had won at first. It took several readings of the fine print before he could determine that was not the case. Unfortunately, because the terms of winning were spelled out in the mailer (albeit not so clearly), no cause of action could be made against the company. So first things first — you have to have an addressable wrong.

The Statute of Limitations Begins

From the day the wrong occurs, the Statute of Limitations clock begins to tick. Again, waste no time in determining what your time limit is, as some are as short as one year. Again, this clock begins ticking when the incident in question occurs, not from when you begin preparing to or actually file suit.

Collecting and Preserving Evidence

When an incident occurs, it is important to keep your head, no matter how upsetting the incident may be. This is where clear thinking pays dividends. It is critical to document as best you can any and all evidence that may be used to support your side of the situation. This extends to filing a detailed police report, amassing any pertinent medical or other reports that are taken by professionals in the event of an accident, recording details using digital cameras, video or even a cell phone if it can download photographs, either at the scene or as quickly as you can return from it. Collect all the documents you possess that pertain to the incident. See Chapter Five, Pretrial Preparation for more on this. Documents you do not have access to, such as papers that belong to the opposing party may be accessible through the Discovery process discussed in Chapter Five.

Demand Letter to the Defendant

A **Demand Letter** consists of your version of the facts outlining your theory of liability (why the other side is responsible), and your claim for damages, supported by all the medical records on which you base your claim. (See Appendix A for a sample letter.) Do not leave anything out, even — especially — something you consider to be especially ambivalent or even bad for your case.

Negotiations

Negotiations begin in an attempt to reach settlement. At this point, you should already know what you are seeking in terms of reparation and what you are willing to settle for (not always the same number). These amounts should rest on the liability situation, namely, clear, probable, and based on your **special damages** — your past medical bills, future medical expenses, lost wages, lost earning capacity, and any expenses incurred to obtain medical care or while you are incapacitated, including child-care expenses. The calculation of your **pain and suffering** is a multiple of the total of these (three or four times, for example), depending on the seriousness of your case. Defendants and insurance companies are less likely to settle unless liability is clear or damages are significant.

Offer of Settlement (also known as Offer of Judgment)

An **Offer of Settlement** is an offer made in writing to settle a lawsuit for a specific sum that comes with consequences. Different States have different rules. In some States, only the Defendants can make such offers. In other States, both sides can. Many States allow as few as ten days in which to respond to the offer; Oregon, for example, allows only three days. All allow the taxing of costs as the penalty for refusing a reasonable offer. Several States, including Florida, include attorney fees.[1] Your Court's Rule Book will provide you with the rules governing Offers of Settlement.

In Florida, for example, the Defendant may serve an Offer of Settlement/Judgment on the Plaintiff 90 days after commencement of the action (i.e., the actual filing of the lawsuit). The Plaintiff has 30 days to accept. If he fails to accept the offer and the ultimate verdict is zero or at least 25 percent less than the offer, the Plaintiff is liable for the Defendant's reasonable costs and attorney fees from the date of service of the offer. The Plaintiff may serve a Demand for Settlement/Judgment on the Defendant no sooner than 90 days after service of process, i.e., after the date the Defendant is served with the Complaint. If the Defendant fails to accept within 30 days, and if the verdict is at least 25 percent greater than the offer, the Defendant is liable for the Plaintiff's reasonable costs and attorney fees from the date of service of the offer.[2]

---

[1] Survey of State Offer of Judgment Provisions. 6 Jan. 2005. American College of Trial Lawyers. 12 Sep. 2010. <http://www.actl.com/AM/Template.cfm?Section=All_Publications&Template=/CM/ContentDisplay.cfm&ContentFileID=53>.

[2] Fla. Stat. §768.79 ; Fla.R.Civ.P. 1.442

Filing Suit

If you are not able to settle the lawsuit reasonably, such as when the other side offers you nothing, then it is time to file suit. Also, as we have discussed before, if your Statute of Limitations is about to run out of time, you have no choice but to file suit. Reminder: if you are close to the end of your Statute of Limitations expiration date during negotiations, you should file regardless as to whether you hope to receive an acceptable settlement soon. It would be frustrating to discover the Statute of Limitations had expired while you were still negotiating, leaving you with no recourse to pursue your claim.

As discussed previously, it is very important to ensure you are filing your suit in the appropriate Court. The Clerk's office can be very helpful here, but don't wait — it is always best to do your research beforehand. At the very least, you won't feel quite so lost when you enter that busy, imposing Courthouse to file your suit. Make sure you have your filing fees ready in the form of payment acceptable to that Court. A simple phone call to the Clerk's office several days before you plan to file can save you time, frustration and potential embarrassment.

Defendant Files an Answer (or Motion)

Within typically 30 days of having been served with a Complaint, the Defendant is required to file an **Answer**. The Answer contains the Defendant's responses to the factual allegations, any **Affirmative Defenses** the Defendant may have, and any **Counterclaims**. The Defendant must either admit or deny each allegation individually or file a **General Denial** of all of them. If the Defendant fails to admit or deny some or all of these allegations, any and all allegations not responded to are deemed to have been admitted by the Defendant by default.

If, as a Defendant, you find you need more time to file your Answer, the Courts are generally fairly accommodating concerning requests for an extension to file. This must, however, be done in accordance with the Court Rules. Check your Rule Book for guidelines on what is required in order to properly file for a **Motion for Enlargement of Time**. In lieu of an Answer, a Defendant can elect to file a **Motion to Dismiss** on technical grounds.

Default Judgments

If the Defendant fails to Answer within the time allotted, the Defendant is judged to be in **Default**. This Default results in automatic admission of all the factual matters contained in the Plaintiff's lawsuit, at which time the Plaintiff files for a **Default Judgment**. All that is required is for the Plaintiff to prove that the Complaint was properly filed and served on the Defendant and that the Defendant failed to Answer, evidenced from the Clerk's original file.

Pretrial Procedures

In the event that the case proceeds to trial, pretrial procedures now begin, including Discovery, Interrogatories, Requests for information, Depositions, Motions, etc., as explained below.

Discovery

During **Discovery**, the Plaintiff and Defendant serve various requests on each other to discover facts and uncover documents and other forms of Evidence in order to learn as much as possible about the opposing party's case. Each of these discovery methods has a specific time limit within which to answer, depending on the Court that has jurisdiction. Check your Court's Rule Book for both the time limits and the permissible scope of Discovery.

Interrogatories (written questions to a party to be answered under oath) are prepared in advance. Generally, anything reasonably calculated to lead to the discovery of admissible Evidence is acceptable.

A **Request to Produce** is a written request to the opposing party to produce documents and/or items related to the case.

A **Request to Admit** is a written request to the opposing party to admit facts above and beyond what was admitted in the Complaint or Answer.

Depositions are where one party questions the other party in person under oath prior to the trial. Lawyers typically refrain from making objections during depositions except when objecting to how a question has been phrased. If the other lawyer instructs the witness not to answer your question, you can suspend the deposition for a ruling by the judge. (This is not a common occurrence.)

Motions, Memoranda and Other Official Documentation

Accompanying all Motions must be a **Notice of Motion**. A date, time and place must be prearranged with the Court Clerk for which to hear the Motion (some judges prefer that you deal directly with their scheduling secretaries or clerks rather than the Court Clerk). This information along with a description of the accompanying Motion must appear in the Notice of Motion. The Court Rules will list any additional documentation potentially required, including any possible **Memorandum of Law**. (See page 48 for more information.)

A Defendant can file a **Motion to Dismiss for Failure to State a Claim** prior to trial, alleging that the Plaintiff's Complaint fails to state a valid claim against the Defendant, (even if everything alleged against the Defendant is true. If the Plaintiff is judged to have failed to state a valid claim, the Plaintiff is granted the opportunity to rewrite his Complaint.

A **Motion to Compel** can be filed in the event you encounter objections by the opposing party to provide answers and/or documentation. This motion asks the Court to compel the other side to respond. It is advisable to research such a motion and provide a **Memorandum of Law** to support such a request, even if the Court Rules do not require one.

A **Motion for Protective Order** asks the Court for the party to be protected from answering the other party's questions. Objections typically revolve around privileges such as the attorney/client, psychologist/patient, and attorney work product.

A **Motion for Summary Judgment** can be filed to request the Court make a judgment based on the fact that evidence or a lack of evidence reveals no genuine issue to merit continuing the lawsuit. This motion can be filed by either Defendant (in the event the Plaintiff hasn't made his case) or Plaintiff (in the event that the Defendant has not provided sufficient evidence to refute liability and justify a trial).

28

A **Motion for Continuance** is a request for more time to prepare and used in almost any situation where there is a hearing or trial set. There must be good justification for granting a continuance and easier to obtain if the other side does not oppose it. Reasons for a continuance can be personal as well as professional, such as in the event of illness, surgery, death of a family member, etc.

A **Motion in Limine** is a request to prevent the admission of a particular fact or piece of Evidence into a proceeding on the grounds of relevance and/or undue prejudice.

Court-Ordered Mediation is a court-mandated attempt by the Plaintiff and Defendant to negotiate their case in good faith without going to trial. It is not a requirement that the case be settled; merely an attempt to reach a mutually agreeable solution if possible. Mediation is especially prevalent in family law cases. Attorneys for both Plaintiff and Defendant are permitted to attend with their clients. The mediator is a court-certified professional, often a lawyer or retired judge.

A **Pretrial Memorandum** is a document generally drawn up prior to the pre-trial conference, often jointly by both Plaintiff and Defendant, to stipulate to as many facts as possible before the trial in order to simplify the trial issues and expedite the trial itself. It may include lists of witnesses, lay and expert; exhibits/evidence that each side intends to present; what depositions, if any, will be read during the trial, all facts agreed upon by both sides, and those issues still in dispute, both factual and legal, on which the case is to be tried.

Jury Charges, also known as jury instructions are compiled prior to the Pretrial Conference as well. Depending upon the Rules of the particular Court, the Plaintiff and Defendant may be asked to submit proposed instructions they would like given to the jury before deliberations begin.

A **Verdict Form** must be provided at the Pretrial Conference for jury trials. The Plaintiff generally draws up this form and presents it to the Defendant. It outlines the precise question(s) that the trial addresses (such as guilt of a crime in a criminal case) and ends with the formal, standard-worded verdict, as dictated by the Rules of the Court, to be decided upon by the jury and read aloud by the jury foreman when the jury has reached a decision.

A **Trial Brief** may be prepared by either side to address any remaining unanswered issues, specifically matters of law, following the Pretrial Conference. This includes questions regarding the opponent's proposed jury instructions and any unresolved matters of Evidence. Appropriate case law and/or statutes should be cited in the brief to support the issue(s) in question.

The **Pretrial Conference** is a meeting of the parties with the judge, held shortly before the trial, to review each side's case with the Court. All outstanding motions are likely to be heard and ruled on at this conference, as well as reviewing the proposed jury instructions and the verdict form. The Court will request an estimate of the trial's duration and may schedule the trial date immediately. Alternatively, Plaintiff and Defendant will be notified subsequently as to the scheduled trial date.

A **Pretrial Order** containing all the rulings, stipulations and other matters decided is drawn up following the Pretrial Conference. This order is the guide that the Court and the parties follow throughout the trial. One party may be requested to draw it up for the other's approval and submission to the Court.

CHAPTER
5

PREPARING FOR TRIAL STEP BY STEP

From the moment you begin thinking about bringing a possible lawsuit or when an incident occurs that would necessitate one, you should immediately begin preparing your trial notebook. Your trial notebook is a navigation tool. It will be your procedural road map; how you will chart your way through the case. It is a fluid system that you will use throughout your preparatory work, continually adding and amending as needed. Your trial notebook will accompany you throughout all the preparation stages as well as the trial. You will store inside it copies of every piece of documentation concerning your case, including your notes and any briefs and memoranda you draft.

It is also advisable to *keep an additional spiral pocket notebook with you at all times* to jot down notes and thoughts as they occur to you. Keep it on your bedside table every night, along with a pen. Every time you have a thought about the case, jot it down in your notebook. Flashes of inspiration come at the oddest times. Some of your best ideas for your Opening Statement or Closing Argument might come to you at the bus stop. Brilliant questions might pop into your mind when you are in the grocery store. You need to be prepared to note these as soon as they occur to you. If you wait until you get home, you might easily forget. And then it will be too late. Transfer these notes to your trial notebook daily.

Ideally, all your preparations may mean you never need to go to trial if you can settle or receive a summary judgment from the judge. Getting organized from the very start is the most effective method to ensure a swift and (hopefully) agreeable resolution. *Representing Yourself* will take you step by step through the best way to prepare your lawsuit, if you decide to represent yourself.

Start by purchasing a sturdy loose-leaf binder two or three inches thick, which will not only provide plenty of expansion room but permit you later on to shift sections as necessary. Dividers with erasable or removable tabs are recommended so that sections can be amended or adjusted during your preparations. Additional page pockets, particularly those that can be tied closed or otherwise secured are also handy for small items that cannot be (or you prefer not to have) three-hole punched, such as reprints of photographs. Clear plastic sleeves that open at the top and provide pre-punched holes to accommodate a binder are another helpful tool. Inside these, you can store multiple copies of the same document for easy retrieval during trial or at filing, when you need to produce for the Court more than one clean copy at a time.

Note: Any original documents, photographs or other important pieces of Evidence should be kept in a safe place, never inside your trial notebook. Your trial notebook should only contain photocopies of documents and Evidence so that you can jot notes on them for yourself while maintaining clean originals for both the trial and the County Clerk's file.

Your trial notebook should have sections for every evidentiary issue that may come up both before and during the trial as well as each evidentiary point that you need to make during the trial, with notations of which witnesses and which documents or other pieces of Evidence support that point. It needs to also have sections for each witness you expect to call or that you expect the other side to call. Finally, you need to have a place to make notes for your Opening Statement and Closing Argument.

Generally speaking, this list is a good starting point for labeling your dividers:

- Demand Letter *(Plaintiff to Defendant)*
- Defendant's Response to Demand Letter
- Offer of Settlement *(if any)*
- Complaint *(filed by Plaintiff)*
- Answer *(filed by Defendant)*
- Motions-Plaintiff *(filed by Plaintiff)**
- Motions-Defendant *(filed by Defendant)**
- Preliminary Negotiations
- Evidence *(Plaintiff's vs. Defendant's)*
- Depositions*
- Witnesses *(lay and expert; Plaintiff's vs. Defendant's)*
- Pretrial Briefs*
- Pretrial Memorandum *(prior to pretrial conference)*
- Jury Instructions Draft *(proposed instructions to present at pretrial conference)*
- Verdict Form *(Plaintiff only)*
- Pretrial Order *(rules governing your specific trial; decided in pretrial conference)*
- Opening Statement
- Closing Argument

*If the proceedings are complicated or require multiple briefs and/or motions, these sections may benefit from being subdivided.

Each section should include several blank pages right from the start to jot notes.

First Things First

There are a few important pieces of research that you should begin with first, before you even start collecting Evidence, initiate negotiations, etc. (The exception to this is if your lawsuit was spurred by an incident such as an accident where, if you were not able to take photographs at the scene of the incident, you must return as soon as possible to do so, particularly where items such as skid marks or Evidence that may not remain intact for any period of time are factors. See Chapter Six, Collecting and Preserving Evidence for more on this.)

The first thing to determine is what Court will have jurisdiction over your potential lawsuit. If the incident that has sparked your lawsuit did not occur in the county of your residence or place of business, then you must verify what **Venue** (location) applies. If the Defendant either resides or does business in the County in which you are bringing your lawsuit or that the facts that make up the basis of your suit occurred in that County, then you can proceed with that County Court. If the Defendant does not reside or work in your County and the incident did not take place, you might have to sue the Defendant in another County. Ask your County Clerk.

The type of Court may vary by type of lawsuit as well as amount of damages. Again, ask your County Clerk who should be able to advise you.

If the Clerk tells you that your home County has jurisdiction and indicates, based on the type of case you have and any estimate of damages (such as for Small Claims Court), the type of Court, you must then ask the Clerk:

1. Where you can immediately purchase a Rule Book for that Court;
2. To clarify what type of case you have (if you are unsure) so you can find out the Statute of Limitations that applies to you; and
3. The location of local law libraries where you can perform your research, if needed.

Now that you know the Court for your case and have rushed out and purchased the Court's Rule Book, check the Rule Book for the particular Statute of Limitations that applies to you. This is potentially critical if time has elapsed since the inciting incident. You need to know precisely how much time you have left to file a Complaint and initiate your lawsuit. *If the expiration is approaching fast, you will make filing your Complaint your first agenda item.* If you have, for example, months or even years before it expires, then you can proceed with negotiation attempts before ever needing to formally file your Complaint.

From this point, we will proceed on the assumption that you do not have to rush out and file your Complaint. (If you do, skip down to the Complaint section and then return to this point once you have filed your Complaint.)

Pretrial Preparations

Pretrial preparation begins on Day One ideally. Suppose you are in a car accident. Obviously, the very first thing you should do is make sure you are all right, that you take care of yourself. Then, you make sure the other driver is okay. Document your injuries with the EMTs if they are called, no matter how minor or insignificant they may seem at the time. If EMTs are not on the scene, do so with the police officer that responds. Don't rely on the police department to look out for your interests. You must request a copy of the police report right away.

Take photographs of the scene, ideally with a digital camera or your cell phone (if it can download photos) at the actual time of the accident (date stamps are handy here if your phone or camera has the capability). Otherwise, return to the scene and take them as close to the time of the accident as possible. Measure any skid marks, noting which vehicle they correspond to. Collect all your medical records. Do not forget the ambulance report, if any. Be sure to share *all* your symptoms, even if they're no longer bothering you, to *everyone* who examines you. This may sound like a no-brainer, but at the accident scene, you may not be feeling your injuries quite yet. Sometimes the more serious discomfort develops hours later. It is best not to say you are okay if you think you may be injured. Go ahead and say that you may be injured. Otherwise, the other side will use your initial statement that you were not injured against you at the trial.

The secret to negotiation is never be afraid to walk away from the table, but you need to decide ahead of time what you want and what you are willing to settle for (not always the same number). Of course, this only works if your numbers are reasonable, based on the liability situation, namely, clear, probable, and based on your **special damages** — your past medical bills, future medical expenses, lost wages, lost earning capacity, and any expenses incurred to obtain medical care or while you are incapacitated, including child-care expenses. The calculation of your **pain and suffering** is a multiple of the total of these (three or four times, for example), depending on the seriousness of your case. This is not to say that you should not negotiate in good faith – you absolutely should. But at this stage, discovery is ongoing and Defendants and insurance companies are less likely to settle unless liability is clear or damages are very bad.

It should be noted that any and all correspondence that is made between Plaintiff and Defendant outside of Court filings (i.e., attempts to address and negotiate the case before a formal Complaint is filed with the Court), should be sent certified mail, return receipt requested, for recordkeeping purposes.

Many of the forms discussed here can be obtained through the County Clerk's Office, paralegal form filing services, photocopied at local law libraries, purchased at book stores where legal forms are sold, and even on the Internet. If using the Internet, ensure that the form you are using is acceptable in your State. The County Clerk's Office can help you with this.

As a Plaintiff, the next step is to draw up what is known as a Demand Letter to the Defendant. As explained in Chapter Four, this consists of your view of the facts outlining your theory of liability (why the other side is responsible), and your claim for damages, supported by all the appropriate medical records, estimates, etc., upon which you are basing your claim. In Appendix A, you will find a sample letter from which to base your own. Do not omit any facts, including those that may appear potentially unimportant or even bad for your case. Keep emotion out (as you should in all your filings.) This is a place to state the facts, explain why you feel the other party is liable, and detail damages.

At this point, assuming you don't need to rush and file your Complaint ahead of the Statute of Limitations expiration, negotiations should begin. An Offer of Settlement may be drawn up and sent to the Plaintiff. If the Defendant refuses to offer settlement, negotiate or even respond to your Letter of Demand, it is time to file your Complaint.

Complaint

Your Complaint is the document in which you must set forth all the elements of your **Cause of Action** against the Defendant. A sample Complaint appears in Appendix B.

Your name, address, telephone and any fax number must appear and you must indicate that you are proceeding Pro Se. You can do this in several different ways. You can place it at the beginning, in the top left corner of the first page, or at the end, bottom left corner of the last page. If you put it at the end, you still may identify yourself as the Plaintiff, proceeding Pro Se, in the first paragraph.

Next, you need to have your **Style of the Case** or **Caption** which sets forth the Court, the parties, the Case Number (to be assigned to your Complaint by the Clerk's Office), the name of your **Pleading** (the paper filed by a party to a suit containing claims or defenses; in this case, the name of your Pleading would be "Complaint") and, if you wish one, that you demand a jury trial. In negligence cases, juries are almost universally demanded.

Then you list your factual allegations. First, you must establish **Venue** (i.e., location), namely, show that the Defendant either resides or does business in the County in which you are bringing your lawsuit or that the facts that make up the basis of your suit occurred in that County, to establish that the Court can exercise jurisdiction over your case. You can make a separate allegation for this, or it can be contained in the allegations of wrongdoing, such as when the venue depends on the wrong having occurred in the subject County.

You must thereafter "plead" enough facts to support your claim. You can use any number of legal form books, some of which may be available at your local law library. Numerous examples of Complaints of all sorts are also available on the Web, but before relying on something you source from the Web, be sure you understand the requirements for your State and County. It is important to note here that less can certainly be more. You are not required to show your hand by delineating all your Evidence, but just to allege enough to make your claim. Do your homework. Some States, notably, New York and California, require very detailed Pleadings.

Next in your Complaint comes your **Prayer for Relief**. It means "request for relief" and derives from historical times when the Courts were highly influenced by the Church. In a negligence case, you are likely asking for money as your form of relief, and you also likely going to include asking for a jury trial as well. (Alternatively, you can make your request to have a jury trial at the end of your Pleading – there are several ways to do it.) Lastly, you will sign your Complaint.

A Defendant can file a **Motion** after being served that alleges that the Plaintiff has failed to state a claim on which relief can be granted. The Defendant can also allege that the Plaintiff filed in the wrong Court or that the Defendant was not properly served with process. It merits cautioning that, if your case is dismissed for technical reasons and your Statute of Limitations runs out while you are trying to fix the technical problems raised by the Defendant before refiling, *you lose.* End of story.

Filing Your Suit

When it is time to head down to the County Clerk's office to file your suit, it's important to be prepared. Before you go, be sure to telephone and find out how much the fees are and what forms of payment are acceptable. Verify with the Clerk precisely what documents you are expected to provide, so you don't overlook anything.

If you are preparing your own Complaint or, for that matter, any paper to be filed with the Court or given to the judge, make sure it is typed and not handwritten, so the judge can read it easily. You have enough to worry about as a Pro Se litigant without having your papers misread.

You must bring the original **Complaint,** which the Clerk will keep on file in the County Clerk's office. (This file will contain every single court-filed document concerning your case, both from Plaintiff and Defendant. You are entitled to request copies of anything you might need but do not have or have misplaced.)

In addition to the original Complaint, you must bring a clean copy for every one of the Defendants listed on the Complaint. (If there are three Defendants, for example, you must bring the original plus three copies of the Complaint with you.) The additional copies are referred to as service copies, meaning each Defendant will receive one when served with notice of the lawsuit you have filed.

Bring yet another clean copy for yourself. Make sure the Clerk stamps the date and time on your copy as well as the original and the service copies. You then take your copy home with you.

In addition, you will need to obtain or prepare both a **Summons** and a **Return of Service,** one for each Defendant. This is because, when the sheriff or other server serves the lawsuit on the Defendant, the sheriff signs the Return of Service after writing the day, date, and time of service on it and sends it back to the Clerk's Office for the Clerk's file. Again, samples of these forms may be found at the Clerk's Office or even on the Internet. Paralegal form filing services can also provide copies for you.

The Summons tells the Defendant the reason for being sued. It contains the **Style of the Case**, i.e., the full names of both parties and the case number that will be assigned to the suit by the Clerk's Office when you file. It also contains contact information for any Plaintiff's lawyer and, most important, the deadline for the Defendant to serve an **Answer** (the response to your Complaint against the Defendant). Usually, this is 30 days from the date on the return of service. Your Court Rule Book will tell you the deadline that applies to you so you can include it.

After ten days from the day you dropped off the copies of the complaints to the Clerk, check with the Clerk's Office every few days to see if the Defendant has been served. If the procedure is such that the return is sent to you instead of directly to the Clerk, you need to file it with the Clerk's Office within the time set forth in the Court Rules. If you can serve the Summons and Complaint yourself using certified mail, you will subsequently need to file the returned proof of service with the Clerk's Office yourself.

Summary of what to bring:

- Original Complaint
- Copies of Complaint for each Defendant plus one for yourself (to be dated by Clerk)

- Summons for each Defendant
- Return of Service for each Defendant
- Acceptable form of payment

DEFENDANT FILES ANSWER

As a Defendant, you have a specified number of days in which to respond to the Plaintiff's Complaint, as indicated in the Court Rule Book and reflected in the Summons.

The Defendant has several options available in the way of a response:

- The Defendant can admit to all the allegations and proceed to settlement.
- The Defendant can file a Motion for Enlargement of Time if additional time is required to craft the Answer. *(See Court Rule Book for requirements.)*
- Defendant can file a General Denial to deny all allegations or selectively admit/deny individually. Note: any unaddressed allegations are deemed to have been admitted, so be sure to address them all if you do not intend to admit culpability.
- Affirmative Defenses.
- Counterclaims (compulsory or permissive).
- Third Party Complaint (Defendant sues a third party).
- Cross-Claims (Defendant makes a claim against another Defendant in the case).
- Motion to Dismiss (if Defendant feels the Plaintiff has failed to make a case).

Unless the Defendant files for and is granted a **Motion for Enlargement of Time** (an extension to file the Answer), failing to answer within the time allotted means the Defendant is said to be in **Default**. This Default results in automatic admission of all the factual matters contained in the Plaintiff's lawsuit.

Affirmative Defenses, where the Defendant admits the allegation but offers a defense for said circumstances or actions, *must* be made in the first responsive Pleading (Answer) or they are lost. (Some Courts may let you add some later for good cause shown but consider that the exception and not the rule. Be sure to include every affirmative defense applicable.)

For instance, one of the most common Affirmative Defenses in negligence cases is that of "contributory" or "comparative negligence." The theory is that the Plaintiff was negligent and the Plaintiff's own actions contributed in whole or in part to the alleged injuries, therefore, precluding recovery at least to the extent of the Plaintiff's own negligence.

This is an important defense to understand as well if you are the Plaintiff in a negligence case. The States are split on this issue. Some States are what we call "pure contributory negligence" States, which means that if the Plaintiff is found to be responsible for even one percent of the negligence, he loses, while others are "pure comparative negligence" States. Whether you are a Plaintiff or Defendant, do your homework. For example, Florida is a comparative negligence State.

Counterclaims are any Causes of Action the Defendant might have against the Plaintiff, whether they relate directly to the present lawsuit (**Compulsory Counterclaim**) or not (**Permissive Counterclaim**). If, as a Defendant, you are making a Compulsory Counterclaim, note that it must be brought up in the first Pleading (Answer) or it is lost to you forever. The Defendant may elect to sue a third party by use of a **Third Party Complaint**, if the Defendant contends that the third party is the real or contributing cause of the Plaintiff's loss. Finally, when there are two or more Defendants in a case, they may make claims against each other, called **Cross-Claims**.

Default Judgments

If you are the Plaintiff, keep a close eye on the time that the Defendant is allotted to file his Answer. Again, unless the Defendant is granted a **Motion for Enlargement of Time** (an extension to file the Answer), failing to answer within the time allotted means the Defendant is said to be in **Default**. This Default results in automatic admission of all the factual matters contained in the Plaintiff's lawsuit.

In the event this occurs and the Defendant fails to answer, the Plaintiff's next step is to file for a **Default Judgment**. All the Plaintiff has to prove is that the Plaintiff properly filed and served the lawsuit on the Defendant and that the Defendant failed to Answer, which the Court can see as evidenced from the Clerk's original file. Ideally, the Plaintiff should prepare a typewritten **Order** (in this case the Default Judgment) beforehand, outlining the facts on which the judgment is based (the facts alleged in the Plaintiff's lawsuit) and granting the Plaintiff a judgment in the amount the Plaintiff is seeking. That way, the judge can sign it immediately and the Plaintiff's case is resolved far more speedily.

Collecting on a Judgment

As the Plaintiff, collecting on a judgment is exactly what it sounds like — collecting whatever damages/reparations were sought in the original complaint. Collecting on your judgment can be achieved in several ways. Obtain or prepare the appropriate pleading. First, you have to serve it on the Defendant so the Defendant knows it has been entered. Then, ideally, you sit and wait for the Appeal time to run out. It differs depending on the Court you are being adjudicated in, particularly Federal versus a State Court.

If the Appeal period has expired and you have not received payment, you may want to try sending a demand letter, threatening sanctions. You do have options if the Defendant ignores you. For example, you may be able to garnish the Defendant's wages. You need to verify your particular State's rules on if, how and when you can do this. The Sheriff can potentially seize the Defendant's property and assets on your behalf. It pays to prepare by doing the necessary research in your State in advance to determine how and when to use these and other possible collection methods.

Pretrial Procedures

Discovery

Once the case has been filed, pretrial **Discovery** begins. During this time, the parties are allowed to serve several papers on each other to discover facts and uncover documents and other forms of Evidence. Whether Plaintiff or Defendant, the first thing you want to research with regard to Discovery is how long you've got. Here again, your trusty Court Rule Book will tell you. Keep track in your Trial Notebook of when this starts and when it must end!

During Discovery, **depositions** (asking questions of a witness in person under oath prior to trial) may be taken of any person involved or maybe come involved in the case Thus, you may find yourself in need of the services of a **Court Reporter.** A Court Reporter transcribes the spoken word in depositions, pretrial meetings and the trial itself, as well as any other venue where you may want to ensure you have an accurate transcript of the proceedings. Typically, both sides agree to split the cost of the Court Reporter's presence if it is a trial, hearing, or motion. If one party wants the proceedings to actually be transcribed (typed), that party pays the corresponding fee. If you are taking the deposition of the other party, you pay the costs of the Court Reporter.

Discovery is a critical period of time before a case that should not be squandered. The Discovery period is when invaluable facts about your opponent's case may be revealed to you. You might even discover some weaknesses in your own case and take steps to strengthen your position. Below are the most commonly used discovery requests and explanations on how each can benefit you.

Interrogatories (written questions to a party to be answered under oath)

Although the number of questions you can ask may be limited, the breadth of what you can ask is fairly wide. Generally, anything reasonably calculated to lead to the discovery of admissible Evidence is acceptable. That does not mean, however, that you should waste your virtually free of charge discovery (net of mailing costs) on harassing your adversary. At the very least, remember what was discussed in the etiquette section in the introduction: operate in good faith or it can come back to bite you. A Judge does not look kindly upon harassment attempts.

What you do want to do during the Discovery period is learn everything you can about the opposing party's case and Evidence. Standard interrogatories likely appear in the back of the Rule Book you have purchased, or you can find them at the library or online, but keep in mind that there is also maneuvering room. You can make up your own questions, and you should. You know the intimacies of your case better than anyone. You know what you need to find out. So do not waste this resource; use it, and use it wisely.

If you encounter objections, you might have to file a **Motion to Compel**. This is a Motion asking the Court to compel the other side to answer your questions. You might very well have to research your motion and provide a **Memorandum of Law** with it. You will find a list of common objections that you can make, which can also be made against you, on page 77 under **Cross Examination of Witnesses by the Defendant**. Keep these in mind when crafting your questions.

Be very conscientious about answering Discovery requests of you. Not only can a Motion to Compel be brought against you, with possible sanctions attached, but you could also actually *admit* a fact you did not intend to admit, simply by failing to respond. Once you fail to respond, the Court deems the fact(s) in question to be admitted by you. So it pays to be careful and responsive. Just respond in a thoughtful manner, not in haste.

Requests to Produce

A Request to Produce is precisely what it sounds like: a written request that one party produce documents and/or items to provide the other. With this Discovery tool you can obtain documents that you might not have been able to get otherwise.

For example, let's say your case centers on a contract in dispute. You do not possess the original contract, however the Defendant does. You can force the Defendant to produce the original at a mutually agreeable place and time for inspection and copying. Bingo! You now have a copy of the contract in dispute.

Requests to Admit

A **Request to Admit** can be one of the most powerful tools in your arsenal. Make sure you do not waste any of them requesting information you already possess. You do not want the Defendant to admit the same thing already admitted in the Answer, for instance. Consider them carefully, and make them count. It is important to remember, too, that, if the Defendant fails to Answer these, the facts within are deemed admitted as a matter of law. Check your Rulebook to see if a sample Request to Admit has been provided for your reference. You can also find a sample Request to Admit in the Appendix D on pages 121–124.

Depositions (where one party questions the other party in person under oath)

If you have engaged a lawyer to assist you on an as needed, piecemeal basis, this may be a good time to schedule a consultation. Depositions can be a witness's downfall, if handled knowledgeably and carefully. They must be approached with equal parts caution and risk. You want to thoroughly question your opponent's witnesses without completely giving away your theory of the case. Admittedly, this is probably not so sensitive an issue in the straightforward types of cases you are likely to handle Pro Se. Just make sure you outline each category of questions you want to ask the witness and do not be deterred by anything until you have completed your task. For instance, one line of questions might include whether the witness knows any other person or entity with knowledge or information concerning the incident in question. Then, for each answer you receive, you ask the witness to identify them and detail where you can find them, what they know, how they know it, and so on.

Do not worry if you get an objection from the other side. Lawyers typically refrain from making objections during the deposition except when objecting to how you have phrased a question. Most objections occur during the actual trial. If, during the deposition, you do get an objection, think about what you said, and rephrase your question until you get it right. Do not let the other attorney rattle you. Never lose sight of the fact that you have the right to take this deposition. Also, just because the attorney is objecting, does not mean that attorney is right. Do make sure you understand the objection and try to rephrase your question. If the attorney persists, just instruct the witness to answer. If the other lawyer instructs the witness not to answer your question, you can suspend the deposition for a ruling by the judge. This is not a common occurrence, but it does happen. Being aware is part of being prepared. When you have the option to object during a deposition, be sure you only object when necessary, such as when a question asks for privileged information to be divulged.

Each of these discovery methods has a specific time limit within which to answer, depending on the Court you are in. Make sure you do not let your time to respond expire. Here is where those Rules of Court are crucial. Again, they tell you not only the time limits, but also the permissible scope of Discovery.

Discovery is a very important process and should be taken very seriously. Not only do you need to protect your own rights during the process (see list of objections under **Cross Examination of Witnesses by the Defendant** in Chapter Six), but it is an invaluable opportunity to learn important information about the other side and their case. Here is where that rulebook comes in handy, because it will detail the permissible scope of discovery. That is generally defined as anything that is 'reasonably calculated to lead to the discovery of admissible Evidence' (Fla.R.Civ.P. 1.280(b)(1).) Although it is quite probable that someone has posted the rules for your State online somewhere, there is no guarantee that they are current. Best to spend a few dollars and guarantee your information is accurate and current than take the chance.

Here are some important goals of discovery that you should keep in mind while you are preparing to take and give discovery, and while you are preparing your Trial Notebook.

The primary goals are to:

- obtain relevant, admissible Evidence, such as documents, admissions, testimony and physical Evidence. (Admissible Evidence is that which is actually allowed to be heard, seen and/or considered by the "trier of fact," whether that be the judge or a jury;
- obtain Evidence leading to the discovery of admissible Evidence;
- better understand the basis, both factual and legal, of the opposing party's case;
- identify the opposing party's witnesses, both lay and expert and discover what their testimony is going to be.

- discover what documents or other physical, tangible Evidence your opponent may intend to use;
- use discovery to get to know your opponent, observing style, frustration level and much more, all of which you can use to your advantage;
- weaken the other side's witnesses by getting them to admit facts favorable to you and unfavorable to them.[1]

MOTION PRACTICE

When you prepare to file a Motion, there are several items that should accompany it. In addition to the Motion itself, which presents the details of the issue you want to be decided, is the Notice of Motion, essentially a cover memo to the Court alerting them to your Motion and what it contains. Along with your Motion should be a Memorandum of Law. This is a memo that cites any applicable case law and statues that support your Motion, all of which you will find at the local library.

Notice of Motion

Before filing your Motion, see the Court Clerk (or possibly the judge's own clerk, depending on who handles the judge's calendar) to arrange the date and time of the Motion hearing and list this along with a description of what is to be heard. The Notice should be addressed to the opposing party and contain the **Style** of the case. Generally, that will look something like this:

In the Current Court for the County of (Name of County)
State of (Name of State)
Plaintiff
Case no.
(Name of Plaintiff)
v.
Defendant
(Name of Defendant)

---

1 Schachner, Robert W. *How And When to be Your Own Lawyer*, 2nd ed. New York: The Penguin Group (USA) Ltd, 2003.

It should be titled, "Notice of Motion to Dismiss," or in whatever manner your Court Rules require, and should be signed and dated by you.

The **Memorandum of Law** is something that will require some research on your part so get ready to head to the law library. A Memorandum of Law should accompany any Motion you file and cites case law and statutes that support the points you make in your Motion. Before drafting what should ideally be a single page memorandum, you need to research corresponding case law or statute and then you need to verify the case in point has not been overturned or the statute is still upheld.

In order to check and make sure it is a good law, you do something called "Shepardizing." *Shepard's* is a series of books that should be available in the law library that lists every case and every statute, as well as whether it has been overturned, reversed, or otherwise altered. Check your law against *Shepard's* to make sure it's a law you can effectively cite to prove your point. If not, then you must continue researching until you find a law or case that does make your point that the opposing side cannot argue has been subsequently made invalid.

Now you are ready to write your Memorandum of Law. A single page memorandum is the best idea.

Motion to Dismiss

Before the trial begins, you have several options when seeking relief from the Court. At the very outset of the case, if you are the Defendant, you can file a **Motion to Dismiss** for Failure to State a Claim, alleging that the Plaintiff's Complaint fails to state a valid claim against you (even if everything he alleges against you is true). Of course, you can only use this motion, also called a "demurrer," if the Plaintiff has, in fact, failed to state a claim. Realize he can get the chance to rewrite his Complaint to state one if he can.

Let us say Plaintiff alleges that the two of you were involved in an automobile accident on a specific date, at a specific time, and that he sustained a specified amount in dollars in damages, but he failed to allege any facts to suggest that you had any fault in the accident, for example, that you rear-ended him. This would be a good example of a Complaint that Failed to State a Claim for which relief could be granted.

Motion to Compel

This is a motion that is used during the Discovery process to compel or force your opponent to comply with discovery requests. The best practice is always to try to work things out amicably beforehand through phone calls and letters but, failing that, a Motion to Compel may be necessary. Some or all of the matters in contention may be matters that the other side, especially if represented, has objected to as privileged and, therefore, not discoverable. You need to do your homework again and/or consult legal counsel of your own, especially if the information is crucial to your case. This can happen where the other party is the only one in possession of the Evidence you need to prove an essential part of your case, e.g., photographs taken immediately after the accident that would exonerate you. Be sure to document all your efforts to work the matter out prior to filing the motion. In fact, some Courts require statements from counsel to that effect and some insist it be included as part of the motion. In these matters, your "Memorandum in Support of Motion to Compel" is going to be especially important. The types of issues you face in discovery motions will likely involve matters of privilege, either some direct privilege, such as the attorney/client privilege, or "work product" meaning that the sought after material is the work product of the other side's attorney and is, therefore, not admissible. Work product is essentially any work that contains any thoughts, impressions, strategies or tactics of the opposing attorney.

Motion for Protective Order

In this motion, instead of asking the Court to force the other side to answer, you are asking to be protected from answering their questions. Again, the objections are more than likely going to revolve around privileges such as the attorney/client, psychologist/patient, and attorney work product.

Motion for Summary Judgment

This is a VERY powerful motion, whether you are the Plaintiff or the Defendant. It is typically filed after all or most of the discovery is done and the facts are in. However, affidavits may be filed with the motion to further support it. Fla.R.Civ.P. 1.510 states in pertinent part: "The judgment sought shall be rendered forthwith if the pleadings, depositions, Answers to interrogatories, admissions, affidavits, and other materials as would be admissible in Evidence on file show that there is no genuine issue as to any material fact and that the moving party is entitled to a judgment as a matter of law." This means that, if the Court agrees that there is no "genuine" issue of material fact, you win.

Let's say you are the Defendant and the Plaintiff has proved that you ran into the rear of the vehicle, but has failed to provide Evidence that the collision actually caused any injuries. Because both liability and damages are essential elements of the Plaintiff's case, you may be entitled to a Summary Judgment.

If you are the Plaintiff, you may also file to request a Summary Judgment. It is more difficult in negligence cases because, even if the Defendant admits liability (fault), damages are usually being contested or the parties would never have progressed to a trial.

However, one example of a Summary Judgment for the Plaintiff might be the case of a Breach of Contract. In such a case, the Plaintiff has to prove the fact of the contract with its terms, the breach thereof, and his entitlement to damages from that breach. If the Defendant fails to put up Evidence that raises a "genuine" issue of material fact on both the breach and the damages, the Plaintiff wins. This means that, although he has put up some Evidence, it does not rise to a level that would create a real issue of fact to be decided by a jury and, therefore, the Judgment is granted in your favor.

For a Summary Judgment there are specific rules regarding how much time you have to give the other side to respond. Check your Court's Rule Book.

Motion for Continuance

Motions for Continuance, which are essentially requests for more time to prepare, can be used in almost any situation where you have a hearing or even a trial set. However, you must set forth the reasons to justify the Continuance. Before filing, try to obtain the other side's consent, then make your motion as you would any motion, filing your notice and obtaining your hearing date from the Clerk's Office. If the other counsel agrees to the Continuance, it can be helpful, as with discovery motions, to title the motion, "Agreed Motion for Continuance." That lets the Court know right away that everyone is willing to cooperate.

Sometimes, however, you cannot agree and a hearing will be scheduled. Be sure, as always, that you have documented all attempts to contact the other side and the outcome of each attempt. Also, make sure that your reason is valid, especially if you are asking for the trial itself to be postponed. Sometimes things happen that we cannot foresee: surgery, illness, or death in the family. Even an emergency at your workplace can be sufficient sometimes. Again, do not forget to attach that Memorandum of Law.

Motion in Limine

If you have something that is otherwise not admissible or relevant and is very prejudicial to you, such as the fact that you filed 52 lawsuits before, you can file a Motion in Limine (pronounced LIM-uh-nee) to keep it out. Why use a Motion in Limine to keep out inadmissible Evidence instead of just objecting at the trial? Several reasons. Although this pretrial motion is usually made quite close to the trial, it still affords you the opportunity to file a written Motion, and a Memorandum of Law supporting it. This gives you an extra edge when dealing with inadmissible, particularly highly prejudicial matters. Essentially, any Evidence against you, by definition, is going to be prejudicial to your case. It is the unduly prejudicial that we really need to avoid. And while you already know that you can object to such Evidence during the trial, sometimes the prejudicial nature of the Evidence is so high that you do not want it brought up at all.

Perhaps the fact that the Plaintiff was supporting three adopted, disabled adults on the meager income that you, the Defendant, caused her to lose when you bashed into the rear end of her car is something you do not want a jury to get wind of. What if you had been arrested at age 17? Neither facts are technically relevant to the issues of the case, namely, whether you, the Defendant, caused the accident and, therefore, the lost income. The first piece of prejudicial Evidence would be offered to illustrate the good character of the Plaintiff, but it would still be highly prejudicial. And although there are some times when prior criminal acts are admissible, if you were a juvenile at the time of your prior arrest, the second piece of Evidence should be sought to be excluded.

When you are working on your case, you always need to be thinking about these sorts of things. If something strikes you as unfair, maybe it is something you can keep out with a Motion in Limine. Do your homework. Each State is going to have its standards for what is considered unduly prejudicial, as well as rules for the inadmissibility of other types of otherwise relevant Evidence.

Remember, just because something is relevant does not mean it will ultimately be admissible. This pertains to Evidence too. So be prepared to fight it out if necessary. Motions in Limine are not the only times when you can present written memoranda of law. (See Pretrial Memorandum, Pretrial Conference, Pretrial Order and Trial Notebook.)

Court-ordered Mediation

Many Courts are requiring Court-ordered mediation prior to trial to see if the matter can be resolved without a trial. It is especially prevalent in family law cases. The most important thing to remember here is that you must arrive prepared to negotiate "in good faith." That doesn't mean you have to settle; merely that you have to be prepared to try to come to a mutually agreeable resolution. Attorneys can accompany clients to mediation so do not assume the opposing party will be alone and vulnerable.

Mediation can be a very valuable tool in the pretrial process. During the mediation conference, you can learn new things about the other party's case that may be helpful to you in either preparing your case or in evaluating it for settlement purposes. Several schools of thought exist as to how mediation should be handled. Some people just show up and let the mediator (a Court-certified professional, often a lawyer or retired judge) handle everything. Some people take a more proactive approach. It pays to be proactive.

First, the mediator will detail the rules and goals of mediation. Then the joint session begins. During this time, each party has the opportunity to outline their case to the other party on the theory that this disclosure will foster settlement. Some people lay it all out. I have seen some defense lawyers get downright nasty when talking to Plaintiffs about their cases. Some lawyers think this is an effective ploy; I disagree. There are also those who outline their case, but hold back a few juicy tidbits, not willing to give up their cases completely. That was much more my style, especially if I did not think there was much chance in the case being settled. But whatever your style, the purpose is to get the ball rolling, get talking and try to settle the case, if possible.

After the joint session, you break up into groups, Plaintiffs and Defendants. The mediator then goes back and forth between the rooms, taking offers and counteroffers, if any, and generally doing his best to get the matter settled. Once settled at mediation, the same case cannot be brought back to Court.

Pretrial Memorandum

These are often required to be filed by the parties as a Joint Pretrial Memorandum. The purpose is to simplify the issues for the trial, to stipulate to facts wherever possible, and generally streamline the trial process. The Memorandum can include a list of the witnesses (both lay and expert) that each side expects to call, a list of each party's exhibits, a designation of those depositions in whole or in part that the party intends to read into Evidence, a list of all facts that have been stipulated (agreed) to, and those issues still in dispute, both factual and legal, on which the case can be tried. Once the parties have agreed to as much as possible, they prepare the Joint Pretrial Memorandum (if they can get along well enough to make one; otherwise each side can submit their own).

Jury Instructions/Charges

Besides the Pretrial Memorandum, you are also likely to be asked to submit proposed instructions to the jury. Although the law library may very well have a book of suggested general jury instructions, also known as "jury charges," this may be another time to seek help from part-time counsel.

The jury instructions present to the jury the law on which the case is to be decided. You do not want to miss anything favorable here and you certainly do not want to let anything unfavorable get by you if you can keep it out. One good thing about standard jury instructions, which hopefully your library has, is that they often cite the authority on which they rely. Citations are like footnotes, only much more formal in this setting. You cannot make any statement on the law without a legal citation to back it up. See, for example, *Standard Jury Instructions – Civil Cases*, posted by the Florida Supreme Court and updated in 2010.[2]

You are also likely to be asked to agree on a **Verdict Form** to be presented to the jury. The Plaintiff is generally the one to draw up the form and present it to the Defendant. Again, there are form books and forms on the Web for you to review. The Jury Instructions referenced above by the State of Florida include model Verdict Forms. However, the one for simple negligence is a bit confusing because Florida happens to be a "pure" comparative negligence State, whereas yours may not be. Researching this issue before you even file your Complaint means you will be prepared when it comes time to produce a Verdict Form.

Although there is some redundancy with Motions in Limine, this is the time to do your **Trial Brief** as well. In your trial brief, you can argue anything left unanswered, specifically matters of law. You can speak to your opponent's proposed jury instructions, and any unresolved matters of Evidence. A brief is simply a document containing arguments on the law that is supported by legal authority such as case law and statutes.

---

[2] *Florida Standard Jury Instructions.* 5 Sep. 2010. Florida Supreme Court. 2010. http://www.floridasupremecourt.org/jury_instructions.shtml

Pretrial Conference

The **Pretrial Conference** is a meeting of the parties with the Judge, held shortly before the trial, to review each side's case with the Court. All outstanding motions are likely to be heard and ruled on now. You may even review the jury instruction and verdict form. The Court then asks the parties how long the matter will take to try. Sometimes, the case date is set right then, depending upon how your judge handles the trial calendar. For example, if the judge has a two-week trial calendar and you tell the judge that your trial should not take any longer than two days to try, and the judge has a three-day trial starting that Monday, then you may be put on standby for that Thursday.

Pretrial Order

After the Pretrial Conference, a Pretrial Order containing all the rulings, stipulations and other matters decided is drawn up. It is the guide that the Court and the parties follow throughout the trial. One of the parties is likely asked to draw it up for the other's approval and submission to the Court.

Opening Statement

Your Opening Statement will be the first opportunity you have, either as Plaintiff or Defendant, to tell the jury your story. When you are drafting your Opening Statement is also the time to set up the framework for your Closing Argument by explaining to the jury just what it is you will show them during the trial. The best Opening Statements are simple and to the point. Remember that saying about speeches:

> Tell them what you are going to tell them;
> Then tell them; and
> Then tell them what you told them.

That holds true in lawsuits as well. In Opening Statement you "tell them what you're going to tell them." In other words, you explain to them what your Evidence will show. You will let them know what is coming, what to expect, but do it in a way that shows the jury your side, your perspective, of your case. You are not permitted to argue your position at this stage, but you can share with the jury what *you* think the Evidence will show.

It's a very good idea to write out your Opening Statement. You have a lot to cover and it is important not to miss anything. Here, you will summarize what you believe the Evidence shows by either telling the jury in a conversational narrative, or listing what each witness and each document will illustrate.

For example, you might say, "Ladies and gentlemen of the Jury, your Honor (always acknowledge both when you speak), as you know, I am representing myself today in this case against the X Brand Toaster Corporation for damages. I believe the Evidence will show that these damages resulted from one of their toasters shorting out and setting fire to my kitchen. The Evidence today will show that the toaster was on the counter next to the spice cabinet and that I had just pushed down the lever when the short occurred..."

Alternatively, you could open with, "You will hear from Mr. Neighbor today and he will tell you [X]. You will also hear from Expert, Mr. Remodel, who will tell you [Y]. I will also take the stand and tell you [Z]." A combination of both approaches may turn out to be best for your case. But keep in mind you have a strict time limit in which to give your Statement. Find out ahead of time how much time you have to give your Opening Statement. And then practice, practice, practice. Read it aloud repeatedly until you're comfortable with it. Speak slowly and clearly. Time yourself. You want to be sure you have sufficient time to say all you need to say.

Whatever approach you choose, it is imperative that you realize this is called an Opening Statement for a reason. It is a statement, not an argument. You must not argue your position. Also, be very careful not to discuss any Evidence that might not make it into the record. This could seriously hurt your credibility with the jury and ruin that endgame we talked about earlier.

Do try to find some thread that ties your Opening Statement to your Closing Argument. Even if all you say within your Closing

Argument is, "Remember in my Opening Statement when I told you that I would show [X]?" This is why you cannot afford to tell them they are going to see or hear something that never materializes. You can be sure that the other side will point out how you had promised in your Opening Statement to provide Evidence of a particular detail or incident but then failed to do so. It goes to your credibility as well as the perceived strength of your case. They will take full advantage of your error in their Closing Argument, if you hand them the opportunity.

Although it is best not to read your Opening Statement verbatim, you are not an expert and if it is the only way to get your message across, do it. You want to address the Jury and hold their attention. You want then to listen to you. So you need to make eye contact and you have to read slowly and clearly. Don't rattle off your Opening Statement with your eyes glued to the page, as if it's a race to the finish. You want to engage them, have them focus on you and what you are telling them.

If you think you can manage your Opening Statement without having to read it, then draft yourself an outline to follow and practice. Practice a lot! Make notes on your outline on each category or witness that you want to talk about and be prepared to place your notes atop the podium provided for easy reference while you address the Judge and Jury.

This is one of the most critical times when you want the Jury focused on you. Your story is what is important in this case. Make it count.

Evidentiary Issues

Evidentiary issues are all the points you produce where there may exist an issue as to whether the Evidence will admissible. This could be Evidence that is important to either side, not just yours. You need to be prepared with some law on the point, whether it's supporting your position or negating your opponent's position. All this can be found in the law library. You must be willing to invest the time, roll up your sleeves and doing some studying. If the issue has to do with your Evidence, for instance, whether a photograph of the damage to the rear end of your vehicle is admissible, you need a statute and/or case(s) to support your point. If the evidentiary issue you are looking at is against you, it is just as important to provide statutes or cases in point that refute the Evidence in question so you can keep the Evidence out.

Working with a Trial Notebook throughout your preparation means that you will be ready, organized, with the point of law at your fingertips — literally — you will be ahead of the game. Trying to do all these things at the last minute before the trial can cost you your case.

Many, if not all these points are handled before the trial ever starts: in the Pretrial Conference, in Motions in Limine or in your Trial Brief. However, things can still come up between that time and the trial. If you have anticipated as much as possible, hopefully, you are already prepared for it and have it properly tabbed in your Trial Notebook for quick, easy access.

Again, once you have found your law, you must check it to make sure it is a good law, a law that is upheld. Check your law against *Shepard's* to make sure it's a law you can effectively cite to prove your point. If not, then you must continue researching until you find a law or case that does make your point that the opposing side cannot argue has been subsequently made invalid.

Now that you have checked your cases and made sure that they are all good law and that your statutes have not been repealed, you are ready to write. You want one page for each evidentiary point. Not only does this help you break the case down for yourself, but it also helps the judge when making his decision. Be the party with the law behind you.

Evidence At Trial

Besides the legal issues of whether or not something is admissible, you also need to know *how* to get it admitted. For instance, you might have thirty-seven photographs that tell the complete story of your loss and single-handedly win the case for you, but if you cannot get them into Evidence, you lose. You need to know how to prove each element of your case with the Evidence that you have. What do you have to work with?

Well, you have **Testimonial Evidence**, which is what each witness testifies to under oath either in person in Court or by Deposition.

You also have **Documentary Evidence** (documents), **Real Evidence** (tangible things: contracts, photographs, etc.) and **Demonstrative Evidence** (e.g., maps, photographs, illustrations, animations).

All Evidence must be shown to be relevant, material and competent to be admissible. "Relevance" is simply that the Evidence makes the fact it is offered to prove a little more likely. That a fact is judged to be "material" simply means it relates directly to an issue in the case. "Competence" refers to the reliability of the Evidence.

To get Testimonial Evidence before the trier-of-fact (the Jury) at the trial, you must first get that person to swear or affirm to tell the truth as your State requires. Then you must question them regarding their own perceptions, if they are lay witnesses, or their opinions if they are experts. Unless a matter is stricken from the record and/or the Court tells the Jury to disregard testimony, anything testified to from the Witness Stand is Evidence. This is an important reason to know your objections and have them at your fingertips to be ready at the trial.

Documentary Evidence and Real Evidence require authentication for them to be admissible. As to Documentary Evidence, if the document is not a contract or other form of Real Evidence, a discussion of admissibility is outside the scope of this book. If you find yourself with a document that you must get into Evidence that does not fall under the definition of Real or Demonstrative Evidence, check the rules of Evidence for your State on authentication of such Evidence. Then do a little research into the Best Evidence Rule, the Parole Evidence Rule, and the Hearsay Rule. Each of these is an exclusionary rule that would keep your Evidence out if you run afoul of it.

Real Evidence can be authenticated in three ways. You can show:

- the "chain of custody" (the least likely option),
- you can show a unique item (e.g., the *Mona Lisa*, which is known to the witness), or
- you can show an item made unique by the witness or other (e.g., an engraved silver spoon known to the witness, or an exhibit marked at the beginning of a case by a witness or paralegal).

The chain of custody requires that you demonstrate who has had control of the object from the time of the incident, or other relevant time, until the time of the trial.

Photographs can be either Demonstrative or Real. If a witness testifies to what is in the photograph because he knows the subject matter, the photo is considered to be Demonstrative Evidence. If he is a technician who testifies to the operation of the machine that took the photograph, such as from a traffic camera, it is considered to be Real Evidence.

Demonstrative Evidence illustrates or demonstrates a witness's testimony and is admissible when it fairly and accurately does so. To authenticate such Evidence, you must have the witness identify the map, illustration, etc., and testify that it fairly and accurately depicts the scene or situation on the date in question. You might need the witness to identify individual parts of the exhibit.

Often, at trial, you are directed to present your documentary and photographic Evidence to the Court Clerk to be marked as exhibits before they are shown to the judge. In some jurisdictions you are expected to have already marked your exhibits. Then you may still have to give your exhibits to the clerk, who then passes them on to the judge. Check your bible, the Court Rule Book, for instructions on how Evidence is to be handled so that you are prepared when the trial begins.

Witnesses

In your Trial Notebook, you should have a separate section for each witness that you intend to call in the case, plus sections for every witness that you expect the other side to call.

Writing Direct Examination questions can be difficult and frustrating at times. This may be another good time to get some help from a legal adviser, especially if you are the Plaintiff. You really want your **Case-in-Chief** — your primary case — to come off strong. If you are fumbling with wording and the other side is objecting to how you have phrased your questions, it can really hurt your case.

You have two types of witnesses: Lay Witnesses who are everyday people who are not considered experts in your case; and Experts, people who, through education, training, or other specialized knowledge, have a demonstrated "expertise" in a particular subject important to your case.

Your Lay Witnesses

The majority of your witnesses will fall under the category of Lay Witness. Begin by making a master list of every single question that you think of that you might want to ask them. Later, you will likely pare that list down to the most essential questions to the essential and those that tell your story the best. Each witness will tell a piece of your story. Ideally, you will organize your witnesses and your Evidence to tell that story in the best possible, most comprehensible way. As you determine in which order to present your witnesses and Evidence, you will rearrange the sections in your Trial Notebook accordingly.

When you question your witnesses there may be rules governing how you may phrase your questions. You may not be able to use what is known as the **Leading Question** except in specific circumstances. Leading questions are questions that tend to seek a yes or no answer because the answer to the question was phrased within the question itself. Here are some examples.

"You saw the accident, didn't you?" (leading question)

"What did you see? What happened next?" (non-leading question)

If your witness is not an expert witness (more on that below), he or she is only permitted to testify to his or her direct knowledge of the incident. In other words, he cannot testify to what someone else told him happened, only to what he experienced firsthand through any or all of his five senses. Anything else would be called **Hearsay** and is strictly prohibited. Although there are some exceptions to this rule, they are outside the scope of discussion. It is important to phrase your questions so that they do not elicit answers that break the Hearsay Rule. If you ask the types of direct, non-leading questions such as the one shown above, you should not have any trouble.

Normally a lay witness is not permitted to voice opinions. However, there are times when this is permissible. That is when the testimony involves:

- A person's identity, whether identified by appearance, voice, or otherwise
- A person's sanity
- Quantities, such as speed, distance, and size
- Demeanor, mood, or intent
- Intoxication or sobriety
- Physical condition of health, sickness, or injury
- Ownership
- The value of one's own property
- Identification of handwriting

These are the only times that the Federal Rules of Evidence allow Lay Witnesses to give their opinions. You will need to research your State by reading the Court Rule Book to see if its rules are any different.

Your Expert Witnesses

Expert Witnesses are those used for technical, scientific or specialized matter that is beyond the knowledge base of the average Juror. An expert is someone who, because of their education, training, and/or experience, has developed a certain level of proficiency and/or skill in a particular area or field. Because of this, they can give opinions in Court if the proper foundation or basis for the testimony is laid.

To lay the foundation for expert testimony, you merely need to establish your expert's credentials to give the opinion you wish to elicit from him. If he is a physicist and your questions will be about physics, go through his education, his academic affiliations, his research papers, his employment history. Then you can go through what he has done to prepare to give his opinion. What has he reviewed? Who has he spoken with?

Be aware that anything you give your expert to review to form his opinions thereafter becomes discoverable by your opponent. So do not give him your Trial Notebook or anything you have made notes on (considered to be your "attorney work product"). Your expert witness may very well testify by deposition, so your Trial Notebook section on this person may consist of sections of or even a copy of the entire deposition.

As noted earlier, it is very important to practice reading an expert's deposition in order to ensure you can pronounce all the words and read it clearly and smoothly. It is also permissible to have someone else read the deposition aloud for you, even a friend unconnected to your case. Just make sure they practice it. Have them practice in front of you.

Whoever reads the expert's testimony needs to understand what they are reading, then needs to be able to read it clearly without stumbling, and in a loud enough voice for the jury to hear. Ask your associate to either join you at the counsel table or sit in the witness box where the Expert would sit if testifying in person. Make sure they dress and act professionally as, even though the jury knows this person is not the actual expert, they can still react negatively to a poor performance.

Your Opponent's Witnesses

This section of your Trial Notebook is where you formulate your questions for the other side. This is considerably more difficult than it might sound. Trials are fluid and things change, so your questions may need change, too. Again, the more time you spend preparing, the faster you will be able to think on your feet.

Your Opponent's Lay Witnesses

When it comes to **Cross Examination** of the other side's witnesses, there is actually a lot that is decided upon before the trial. Before the trial begins, you will have taken their depositions and will have their discovery responses to refer to. Using these tools, you can decide what questions to ask under what categories. Write these in your Trial Notebook on each witness's dedicated page as you think of them. You can pare these later to what is really necessary to get in and get out – remember you are on Cross Examination at this point.

Make sure you have enough blank paper in this section because you will also want to take notes during the other side's Direct Examination. Some of your most effective questions will come from those notes during Direct Examination. Just don't rush up and ask that one killer question before any other. You really want to get it right. And that means inserting it at the most logical part of your list of questions for that witness.

Keep in mind also that on Cross Examination you can and should ask **Leading Questions**. You want to control what goes on in that witness box now every bit as much as you did on Direct Examination. Some examples of appropriate leading questions are:

- "You said that the X Brand Toaster was without faults,
- didn't you?"
- "But isn't it true that the X Brand Toaster had a faulty timer?"
- "X Brand Corporation was aware of this faulty timer as early as May 2006, wasn't it?"

Discovery Responses

These are important items to have copied in your Trial Notebook. This way they'll be handy to you at all times and, because they're photocopies and not originals, you can make notes on each. Keep your original unmarked in a separate tab entitled "Original Discovery Responses," in case you need it at the trial to impeach a witness.

Expert Witnesses

You will most likely have taken a deposition from the opposing side's Expert so a copy of this along with all your objections to the statement should be included in the Trial Notebook in their witness section. You must also research the Expert's background for any glaring indications calling into question the witness's expertise and file this here. During the Cross Examination, if the Expert Witness is not physically present and the Deposition has been read instead, you can read your objections if they have not yet been ruled on (most likely they will have been ruled on in advance of the trial).

If the Expert is testifying in person, you will ask him all the questions on your prepared list. You may also have the right to **Voir Dire** (question) the Expert as to those qualifications before the Court accepts him. This is true even if you do this by deposition. You can still have your Voir Dire and object to the Expert's qualifications, knowing that the objection will be dealt with prior to the trial.

Make sure you have done your homework for any Expert testimony, but especially live testimony. You do not want to look like a fool in front of the jury. *Sometimes it takes an expert to understand an expert.* If your opponent is bringing an Expert on hot air balloons, you might do well to talk to another expert on hot air balloons before and possibly again after this Expert's deposition so you do not get surprised by what the other side's expert comes up with. If may cost you a bit, but in the end, it would be well worth it. You do not get surprised, and you know how to question the expert.

Exhibits

This section of your Trial Notebook houses the photocopies of all your exhibits, including photographs and anything that is not flat, like the toaster, as well as photocopies of key exhibits from the other side that you have obtained through the Discovery phase. Always use copies so you can mark them (and because the originals may be going into the Court's file).

A note about original exhibits: unless the other side or the Court objects, there is nothing wrong with using photocopies or reprinted photographs. Just mark them "duplicate" so there's no confusion. If you can't reprint the photos, then have laser copies made so you can see them well. They're also easier to three-hole punch and insert into your Trial Notebook binder. (Reprinted photographs can be slipped into transparent sleeves that contain hole punches.)

You want to be clear on how you get each exhibit, each piece of Evidence into Evidence. Make a note as to which witness, yours and/or theirs, can testify to the exhibit and what they can say. See the earlier section in this chapter, Evidence at Trial, for the foundations you need to lay for each type of Evidence. Once you have done this, organize your exhibits according to the witnesses. If there are any exhibits that you want to keep out of Evidence, think about whether you have any witnesses who can testify against the necessary foundation for that piece of Evidence.

Pretrial Order

The Pretrial Order is your "cheat sheet," documenting everything that has been decided for your trial, including witnesses, exhibits, stipulated facts, etc. If it is not in the Pretrial Order, it is either not going to be included in the trial, or it came up after the Pretrial Conference, at which point those single page Memoranda citing case law and/or statutes that we talked about in Chapter Four now play a role.

Closing Argument

As with your Opening Statement, it is highly advisable to write out at least a draft of your Closing Argument ahead of time. Stock this section with at least a dozen sheets of blank paper to jot notes during the proceedings. You may choose not to write your Argument until the second day of the trial, or you may write it before you write your Opening Statement. It is a matter of style. A lot can change within the day or two of trial so you need to be prepared to amend it. You may very likely still be adding to it throughout the trial, even, perhaps especially, during the other side's Closing Argument, if they precede you.

Once you have written your Argument and read it over several times, you are going to redo it in outline form. It may sound backwards, but it's actually not. Once you have your complete Closing Argument drafted, you will condense it into an outline or bullet points and it is from this abbreviated form that you will actually deliver your Argument. These bulleted points should be short blurbs that are just enough to remind you of what you wanted to say next. You do not want to stare at your notes while you are doing your closing. After all, the Closing Argument is not only your last opportunity to address the Jury but also the time when the Jury is expecting you to summarize the key points of the case for them. You must know what you want

66

to say inside out so you can appear confident and thoughtful. By now, you will know your case thoroughly but the bullet points will ensure that you do not miss making a key point or two during this summation.

In your outline, you will insert copies of the jury charges (instructions) that you finalized in the in Pretrial Conference that you want to cover in the corresponding sections of your Argument. Stock your Argument with clean copies of important Evidence that was admitted into trial if they help you reinforce the points you want to make to the Jury. (Remember: *Never ever* make reference to *any* Evidence that was not admitted into trial.)

If you are permitted to handle the exhibits once they have been entered as Evidence (verify ahead of time, if this is something you wish to do), make sure you arrange for them to be available to you beforehand from the Court. This is the point when you say, "Remember when I told you I was going to show [X]?" You proceed to explain how you showed it

with the appropriate witnesses, exhibits, and experts. It is very important to understand the difference between presenting Evidence and giving your opinion about what it does and doesn't mean. You can only point out that the Evidence does or does not support a particular theory, fact, or set of facts.

In Closing Argument, you also finally get to argue. You are permitted to draw reasonable inferences from Evidence. That means connecting the dots, showing where the Evidence either proves or disproves a fact or facts. You want to talk about each issue of the case and illustrate how those necessary to your case have been resolved in your favor. Make sure you show how the Evidence has proved each element of your case. Do not forget to emphasize the **Burden of Proof**, whether it falls upon you as the Plaintiff or falls upon the opposing party if you are the Defendant.

The Closing Argument is also when you argue the credibility of any witnesses. If there were contradictions, for example, this is when you remind the Jury that the other side's witness said one thing on Direct Examination and another in a deposition or other out-of-court statement, and how this shows them to be less than credible as a witness. Do not, however, *ever* call someone a liar. You do *not* accuse someone of lying on the witness stand and you *never* call them a liar during your Closing Argument. You merely lay the evidence of their contradictions in front of the Jury, pointing out how they said one thing at one time and another at another. You are telling the Jury that you believe they have the intelligence to figure out what that means!

If you can, use visual aids and exhibits as these really help reinforce points to the Jury and help the Jury remember them during deliberations. As a Plaintiff, these can be particularly useful when showing how you arrived at your damages amount, if it includes such items as suffering, which is not an amount rendered by an expert. A blow-up of a highly pertinent exhibit, like the intersection where the accident occurred, can also be very valuable in Closing Argument. Even blow-ups of particular Jury Charges can be helpful if they're key points to your case. You want to draw attention to those points that you feel important for the Jury to remember.

Finally — and this is pivotal — make sure you tell the Jury plainly what you are asking for. Do not count on luck or hope that if you're vague, they'll come up with a figure that exceeds your hopes and dreams. Tell the Jury exactly what you are asking for and how you came up with each figure. If you are asking for some other type of relief, make sure you are clear on what you are asking the Jury to do for you. If they do not understand, the odds are that you won't get it.

CHAPTER
6

THE ELEMENTS OF A TRIAL

Now that you have filed your Complaint, gone through Discovery and Court-Ordered Mediation, prepared your pretrial Motions, Briefs, and Memoranda, participated in the Pretrial Conference and prepared the Pretrial Order, it is time for the trial to begin. One important note concerning your Trial Notebook during trial: whenever you give a document to the Court, you must first share a copy with opposing counsel. There is never an exception to this rule. For example, say you are presenting a Memorandum to the Court during the proceedings. You take two copies of your Memorandum out of your Trial Notebook and give one to opposing counsel, and then politely request to approach the Bench. When permission is granted, you approach in what is called a **Sidebar** and hand your Memo to the Court (either the Judge or the Judge's clerk, depending on your Court's protocol). So make sure you have sufficient copies to distribute before entering the Courtroom!

Voir Dire

Voir Dire (pronounced *vwahr deer*) derives from the French, meaning "to see, to speak." This is the only time during the trial when you are allowed to converse directly with the jurors, asking them questions designed to elicit all sorts of information. This includes any prejudice they might harbor against you, either individually or as representative of a group, e.g., race, religion, gender, profession, sexual orientation, etc. Perhaps the jurors think less of you because you are representing yourself. The idea is to determine which jurors you do not want on your jury and which you hope to retain as the best people to hear your lawsuit. You want to learn which jurors are sympathetic to your type of case. Perhaps they had a similar thing happen to them. Of course, you can be sure your opponent is going to want to keep those people out. You are also going to want to know whether anyone has a problem with awarding money damages for your type of case.

Never forget, not only are you evaluating each potential member of the jury but they are also evaluating you. We talked about good impressions in Chapter Four, under "Preparing Yourself." You want the jury candidates to like you. Be polite. Do not call people by their first names. It is "Mr. Jones" and "Ms. Smith." (Using Mrs. may be preferable if a woman is older and either married or widowed.) Don't alienate them by interrogating them; use a more conversational style. You want allies, not adversaries.

For instance, you might ask the group, "Has anyone here ever known an 'X Brand' toaster to short out?' If anyone raises their hands, you point and ask, "What happened to you, Mr. Brown?" (With any luck you have a seating chart with their names on it.)

Keep it polite, keep it semi-formal, but keep it friendly. Smile, nod, and use positive body language. Remember, any of these people could end up on your jury. Of course, if the case happens to be about something terrible, you might not want to try to come off quite like Susie Sunshine. Play it by ear; get a feel for who your jury is. You are going to be with them awhile.

Different Courts "strike a jury" in different ways. Some let you say which three or six you do not want (always start with twice as many as you think you might need) and some make you go juror by juror and say yes or no. You get three peremptory strikes (this literally means you prevent the other side from using them) for a six-person jury and six peremptory strikes for a twelve-person jury. Be prepared to give a non-discriminatory reason for all your choices.

For instance, a female entrepreneur who tries to load the jury with all women jurors is potentially discriminatory toward men, thereby possibly harming the jury process as a whole when one such large group is underrepresented.

Besides peremptory strikes, you also get an unlimited amount of strikes "for cause." In this case, you must generally ask the Court to excuse a person you believe cannot be fair and impartial and give a legally sufficient basis for your request. For instance, if someone on the jury speaks out during Voir Dire against allowing people to proceed with their cases Pro Se, then that person is obviously unable to be a fair and impartial juror, or so your argument goes. Likewise, if a juror is a relative of your opponent's primary witness, you would strike that person for cause.

Opening Statement

Your **Opening Statement** is your second chance to speak in front of the jury. However, now you cannot have a conversation with them. Now it is strictly about what you want to say. The Opening Statement is the time when you tell your story, simply and to the point. Remember what we said in the previous chapter:

> Tell them what you are going to tell them;
> Then tell them; and
> Then tell them what you told them.

For instance, you could begin with: "I am going to show that the X Brand toaster had a timer which was known to X Brand to repeatedly cause their toasters to short out;" or "I will show you Evidence that a short in the X Brand toaster caused a fire in my kitchen;" or "You are going to hear from Mr. Remodel today, an expert in the cost of kitchen remodeling, who will give you an estimate of the cost to repair my kitchen."

Do not try to make your case in Opening Statement; you are not there to argue it but to just make sure the jury understands it. Also, do let them know what your Evidence is going to show. You will capitalize on this later. But be careful. If you are not sure that you are going to be able to get a piece of Evidence in, and it is not vital to the explanation of your case, do not err and mention it in your Opening Statement.

Direct Examination of Witnesses by the Plaintiff

If you are the Plaintiff, this is when you question your own witnesses, asking them only specific types of questions. For instance, you cannot ask your own witness, "Is it not true that on the night of the full moon, my toaster blew up?" That is what is known as a "leading question" and they are generally prohibited when questioning your own witness, except in certain limited circumstances. A good rule is to just to avoid them on Direct Examination.

To know if a question can be defined as leading you can look at it in two ways. First, a leading question contains the answer to the question you are asking. Second, it tends to seek a yes or no response rather than an answer laced with details.

Ask open-ended questions like:

- "How do you know me, Mr. Neighbor?"
- "On the 27th of August, 2010, what were you doing?"
- "What did you hear?"
- "What did you do next?"

It is important to note that it is perfectly permissible to go over your witness's testimony with them before the trial. In fact, you should. What is never permissible is telling them what to say. Once on the stand, if your witness forgets his or her testimony, you can "refresh recollection." To do this you can use almost anything – a document, a photograph, the toaster. The thing you use does not even have to have been generated by the witness; it just has to help him to remember.

If you intend to use Evidence for any purpose during the trial, always make the showing of walking to counsel table with your pre-marked exhibit, even if counsel waves you away each time. (It is also a good habit not to reciprocate and wave your opponent away, because you never know whether something might have been changed somehow since the last time you saw that piece of Evidence.)

Do not forget yourself when it comes to witnesses. *You are also a witness in this case.* When you are ready to give your testimony, simply inform the judge that you would like to testify for yourself. You enter the witness box, are sworn in (give an oath or affirm that your testimony will be true) and proceed to tell your story. Remember: keep it clear and concise and limit it to what is relevant. The jury does not want to know what you had for breakfast the day of the fire. Just tell them what happened. Treat yourself like any other direct witness.

Expert Witnesses

Expert Witnesses are handled a little differently than other witnesses. The first thing is to establish that your expert is qualified to testify as an expert in the field in which you wish to offer him.

Remember our X Brand toaster? Mr. Remodel was an expert in kitchen remodeling. You want to offer his testimony to demonstrate the legitimate value of your loss. To do that, you first have to offer enough witnesses and other admissible Evidence, such as photographs, to give the expert something on which to base his opinion.

Let's say you have a witness, Mr. Neighbor, who can testify to seeing smoke and who rushed over in time to see the toaster sparking and flames everywhere. Either you or he can identify the charred remains of the toaster. Mr. Neighbor also saw what was left of your kitchen immediately after the fire department got through saving your house. He "authenticated" all your photographs by testifying that was how the kitchen looked at each crucial point in time.

In other words, he testified that the Evidence was, in fact, what it claimed or seemed to be because he saw the kitchen and testified that it looked just as it was depicted in the photographs.

There are other ways to authenticate Evidence besides a witness having seen or experienced the issue in question for himself. (See *Entry into Evidence of Documents, Photographs, and Tangible Items by Both Parties* further in this chapter). You will already have endeavored to get each piece of your Evidence "into Evidence," that is, admitted into

Evidence, before the trial began, through Trial Briefs and Motions in Limine. However, Evidence admissibility issues may still arise, so you need to be prepared.

Now, the first thing you want to do after setting up your Evidence is establish your expert's qualifications, whether based upon education, experience or both. Once you have had your expert testify that he has been a kitchen remodeler for twenty years and has seen dozens of kitchen fires, for example, you then "offer/tender him as an expert."

You want to make sure that you cover all of his specific qualifications: all the qualifications that make him the right person to give this opinion. For example, if your expert is an academic, you might want to cover his education, publications, organizations he belongs to, any experience he might have teaching, that sort of thing.

The other side can then question your expert, limited specifically to his qualifications. This is sometimes called a "Voir Dire of the expert." Or they can simply accept him as an expert. The more qualification Evidence you establish, the better it is for you.

Once your expert has been accepted by the Court, you begin asking him the questions to make your case. In the toaster example, the case is made for damages. But there is a special way to phrase these questions. You have to get all the facts you are relying on for the expert's opinion by using a hypothetical question.

For example, "Given your twenty years as a kitchen remodeler and your experience with dozens of kitchen fires, and based on your review of the photographs from both before and after the blaze and the kitchen in this case, have you formed an opinion as to the cost to repair my kitchen?" When he says yes, and, barring any objections to the form of the question, you say, "And what is that opinion, please?"

This is not a purely hypothetical question because our expert has actual knowledge of many, if not all, of the facts. A better example of a hypothetical question might be where you ask your expert to assume some facts that had been testified to by other witnesses, but to which the expert himself had no personal knowledge.

In the instance of a negligence case, you would say something like, "Doctor, I will ask you to assume that Ms. Smith was driving a yellow

Toyota Camry on September 2, 2010 and that on that date Mr. Jones, driving an orange Ford F150 pickup truck, struck Ms. Smith's Camry in the rear, at about 15 mph. I will also ask you to assume ..." as you lay out the facts that have already been attested by other witnesses.

You get the picture. Once you get your facts lined up, you ask if the expert is able to form an opinion whether such a collision could cause the injuries complained of by Ms. Smith. If the answer is yes, then you can go into the underlying reasoning. Remember, the facts you use in your hypothetical question *must already be in Evidence*, whether in the form of documents, photographs, testimony by witnesses or even the crumpled bumper.

If you get an objection to the form of the question, do not panic. Stop and think about precisely how you phrased the question. If you cannot remember, you can ask to have the Court Reporter read the question back to you. Yes, you can really do this and it does not make you look bad. Rephrase the question and this time get it right. Keep in mind that different States have different requirements. Some may not even require that you lay this foundation first.

Make sure that you have your expert explain any terms that may be "terms of art," any technical or vernacular terms that might be unfamiliar to non-professionals, so the jury knows exactly on what the expert is basing his opinion. If the jury does not understand it, they certainly are not very likely to follow it.

Also, instruct your expert before the trial to look at the jury instead of at you when testifying. It has a much more personal feel and tends to keep them talking at a more conversational level. One trick many lawyers use is to stand at the far end of the jury box while asking their questions so the expert or any other direct witness has to look across to the jury to see them. It means you need to speak up, but that is a good thing, too.

If your expert is coming in person, spend some time together before the trial to review his testimony if you can. You want him to be familiar with your questions and not fumble with his answers because he has not thought them through beforehand. Of course, just as with lay witnesses, you cannot tell the expert witness what to say. I always instruct my witnesses to tell the truth at trial. That way, if the opposing lawyer asked:

> "Did you discuss your testimony with the Plaintiff's counsel last night?"
> The witness would say yes and the attorney grin, practically rubbing his hands together in delicious anticipation.
> "And what did he tell you to say?"
> "He told me to tell the truth." (The grin would then disappear!)

One thing to keep in mind about expert testimony is that frequently it is taken by deposition before the trial, because either many experts are professionals who cannot take off a day to come to Court or you can't afford to pay their fee to do so. This puts you in the position of having to craft your questions very carefully so they do not get thrown out for you having included facts not in Evidence. Whether you finish having to use the hypothetical question form in your State, you still have to lay a proper foundation. Be clear on what that is and have your questions ready.

When you have taken your expert's testimony by deposition, that means you can read the deposition aloud at the trial. You will read the words of the expert and your opponent reads any objections (to the extent they have not already been ruled upon) and questions.

Chances are, you have agreed beforehand as to the how the objections are to be handled or the Judge may have already ruled at the **Pretrial Conference**. Any objectionable content is then blacked out so it is not read to the Jury.

It's advisable to do this on a copy of the deposition so you maintain a clean original transcription. Because you are doing the reading, make sure you understand what it is you are going to be talking about. Make sure you can pronounce all the words correctly and without stumbling. Don't drone on in monotone or race through it too quickly.

This may sound silly, but when you have a technical deposition, it can mean the difference between a jury that cares what you are saying and one that snoozes through it. Practice reading it so you can do so in a more conversational way. This is your expert; he is important to your case so make sure he's heard.

Cross Examination of Witnesses by the Defendant

After you, if you are the Plaintiff, examine each of your witnesses, the opposing counsel has the right of **Cross Examination**. That means the Defendant can question your witnesses, limited to within the general scope of your Direct Examination. In other words, he cannot go into topics you did not cover on Direct Examination.

The other lawyer can do several things on Cross Examination. He can use your witnesses to introduce Evidence. He is not prohibited from asking leading questions because they are not his witnesses, so he can try to emphasize those points which were good for him and then "impeach" your witness, i.e., bring into question the witness's credibility.

Your opponent may attempt to show that your witness could not have seen what he or she testified to because of confusion over the street name; or maybe he will just get the witness to admit uncertainty about the scene. Cross Examination of your witnesses can be one of the most frustrating times during the trial. But you are not without recourse. You can make an objection if you think the question is improper.

Before I talk further about objections, let me give you some very basic guidelines before making any objection that may save you in front of a jury. Ask yourself:

- Is there a legitimate objection I can make?
- Should I make it?

There is nothing worse than making a slew of objections and having the judge overrule you every time in front of the jury. You need to remember that just because a question may be objectionable, if it is not hurting you, does not mean you should make an objection. Here is a list of common objections:

- The attorney is leading the witness; the question is suggestive.

- The question has already been asked and answered.
- The question is argumentative.
- The question or answer assumes facts not in Evidence.
- No proper foundation for the question or answer has been laid.
- The question is unintelligible.
- The question goes beyond the scope of the direct examination.
- The question calls for an opinion by an expert and the witness has not qualified as such.
- The Evidence is barred by the Best Evidence Rule; what is being offered is not an original document.
- The Evidence is not germane to the issues in this case.
- The Evidence is repetitive and has already been introduced.
- The Evidence is immaterial to the case; it does not prove or disprove any material fact.
- The witness is not qualified to testify; the witness is incompetent.
- Hearsay; the witness is not the person involved in the prior out-of-court event.
- The testimony or Evidence is barred by the Fifth Amendment; the witness cannot be forced to incriminate himself or herself.
- The question is compound; it consists of two or more questions.
- The answer is privileged: husband/wife, attorney/client, clergy/parishioner, and so on.

Redirect Examination of Witnesses by Plaintiff

Sometimes you can ask the Court for a brief **Redirect** of your witness, which means that, when the Defendant's lawyer is finished the Cross Examination, you can address your witness again. It is generally limited to the scope of Cross Examination. You want to use this to cover anything the Defendant brought out on Cross Examination that you did not cover or sufficiently cover on Direct Examination, if it is important to your case. Otherwise, leave it alone. The possibility that you might open up something new always exists, and the Defendant would get the chance to Recross, i.e., take their second shot at the witness.

Entry into Evidence of Documents, Photographs and Tangible Items by Both Parties

During your **case-in-chief**, you are concerned with introducing all your Evidence. This is the time you must do it. But what constitutes Evidence? It is the testimony of all the witnesses plus the facts stipulated to by the parties in the Pretrial Order, and all the documents, photographs and tangible things you rely on to prove your case. If you have documents or photographs (do not forget the toaster), then these have either already been agreed to by the parties or you have authenticated them using one or more of your witnesses.

You can do this in several ways: through testimony that a witness had *direct knowledge* of the Evidence, such as where someone was a witness to the contract you have alleged was breached. Also, if some object is unique, your witness can testify that they have knowledge of that object, such as a novel with a note from the author inside the cover.

Or, in the toaster case, Mr. Neighbor can testify that he has seen that toaster before and he knows it is the same one because, while you and he were talking before his testimony, he made a little red mark right next to where the short occurred and the toaster shown the Court bears that same mark. By doing that, Mr. Neighbor made the Evidence unique.

You can also authenticate Evidence by proving **chain of custody**. This means that you have to show where the Evidence was at all times, but it is unlikely in these types of proceedings that you are going to be called on to authenticate your Evidence in this manner.

Be sure you are clear on the rules of Evidence in your jurisdiction. You do not want to get caught not knowing how to get your Evidence before the jury. If it is not admitted into Evidence, the jury cannot consider it in your case.

Of course, your witnesses' testimonies under oath, whether in person or by deposition, are Evidence and need no further authentication. It is unusual but the Court can take **Judicial Notice** of a fact or set of facts that are basically common knowledge. If the fact that slower traffic is supposed to stay in the right lane is important to your case, you ask the Court to take **Judicial Notice** of it.

Sidebars

There are times when the Court will wish to speak to you outside the hearing of the jury. These are called **Sidebars**. Now, you "approach the bench" and lean in to hear and be heard on whatever the matter might be. Most often it is a question of whether a piece of Evidence should be shown to the jury or whether a specific line of questioning should be allowed of a witness.

These are the times that you want your memos ready with case citations supporting the admission of the Evidence, facts or questioning. You have done your job, you have thought ahead, you have done the work and now you are reaping the benefits. Remember, never give anything to the judge that you do not give or at least show to opposing counsel first.

Presentation of Any Evidentiary Motions that Arise during the Plaintiff's Case

This is when **Sidebars** occur. Either party might have an evidentiary issue arise that needs to be addressed. Again, you are ready with your Memoranda of Law as you have anticipated the problems that might come up with some Evidence, his and yours, and done your research.

This is another instance in when having a lawyer review your case could be well worth the fee. Most issues at ths point will hopefully have already been handled via your **Trial Brief and Motions in Limine**. However, you have to be ready.

Make sure you ask to approach the Bench, by politely asking, "Your Honor, may we approach the Bench?" At that point, you first hand a copy of your memorandum to opposing counsel and then hand a copy to the Judge. Make your argument (to either keep the Evidence out or let it in), but be clear and to the point. The chances of you winning on these points goes up dramatically if you have done your homework beforehand and prepared your Memoranda.

Plaintiff Rests His Case

When you, as Plaintiff, have presented all your witnesses, read any and all depositions you needed to into Evidence (such as those of experts) and entered all your other Evidence, you then officially rest your case. This means that you are satisfied that you have put on enough Evidence to prove your case.

Remember, as Plaintiff, the **Burden of Proof** falls upon you. In most civil matters, especially personal injury, you need to prove your case by a **Preponderance of the Evidence**. This means the greater weight of the Evidence. Greater weight is not the same thing as providing the most Evidence. It means providing the most credible, believable Evidence. This could come down to a single document, witness, or photograph (or toaster). Once you have rested, the defense proceeds to put on its case.

Motion for Directed Verdict

After the Plaintiff rests, the Defendant may make a **Motion for a Directed Verdict**. This motion asks the Court to go ahead and rule in the Defendant's favor because the Defendant believes the Plaintiff has failed to properly prove each element of the Plaintiff's case; failed to put on what is known as a **prima facie** case, one that is entitled to go forward "on its face."

This motion takes the case out of the hands of the Jury, so Courts are reluctant to grant them unless the matter is clear-cut. For example, the standard for granting a Directed Verdict in Florida is: "A motion for directed verdict should be granted only where no view of the Evidence, or inferences made therefrom, could support a verdict for the nonmoving party."[1]

However, it is important to make the motion if there is any question that the other party has failed to meet his burden, in order to preserve the issue for **Appeal** (See "Appellate Review" to follow).

---

[1] Soltwisch v. Pasco County, Case No. 2D08-6070 (Fla. 2d DCA 2010), citing Sims v. Cristinzio, 898 So. 2d 1004, 1005 (Fla. 2d DCA 2005)

Direct Examination of Witnesses by the Defendant

This goes for the Defendant just as it did for you, only now you are the one with the right to object to the questions. The same rules apply:

- Is there an objection I can make?
- Should I make it?

Being quiet during your opponent's questioning is not a sign of weakness. However, by all means, object if you need to. Just avoid over-objecting if possible.

For example, if the Defendant's attorney is leading the witness, but only to elicit the person's address and other identifying information, let it go. This is a good example of a time when a question, though it may be objectionable, does not hurt you. That is really the "Should I make it?" standard for objecting. "Is this going to hurt me if I allow it?" It means you have to think on your feet.

Cross Examination of Witnesses by the Plaintiff

Now it is your turn to for **Cross Examination**. You have taken good notes during the Defendant's Direct Examination and you know what you need to ask. Ignore your opponent's style of Cross Examination. I say this because it is always tempting to do return like for like. For your Cross Examination, you need to think like a snake. You are going in and striking, quick and sharp, at each point you need to make. Why? Because the jury is going to remember it.

So what do you need to ask? If they have admitted anything that is good for your case, some people believe it is advantageous to get them to repeat it for emphasis. Just be aware that you risk getting an "asked and answered" objection if you try. It may be more effective to save it for your **Closing Argument**, unless the answer is not complete. Then, by all means, go in and get your Evidence.

If the Defendant's attorney opens the door to a particular line of questioning, even privileged matters, that you want to go into, you may. And if the witness makes a contradicting statement between the prior deposition, interrogatories or any prior out-of-court statement and the answers at the trial, that is your cue to impeach the witness, to attack their credibility.

You do this by getting the witness to repeat what they have just said in trial assertion. Then, you ask if the witness remembers giving a deposition, answering interrogatories, and so on. If the answer is yes, as it will invariably be, ask the Court's permission to approach the witness. *Always* ask permission to approach the witness before doing so. Show first the opposing counsel and then the witness the discovery document and open it to the relevant page. Ask if the witness remembers giving the deposition *under oath.*

Some witnesses are required to sign their depositions and some are not, depending on your jurisdiction, but if the signature is there, have the witness state that it is, in fact, their signature. In some States, you have to give the witness a chance to "refresh their recollection."

In others, you can just ask the witness to read the previous answer into the record or even do it yourself. Voila! The witness is impeached. No need to go further and say, "So the testimony you gave here at the trial under oath today was not correct, was it?" The jury has already realized that. Remember, you are a viper. Strike and get out. You can draw all your little strings together during your **Closing Argument**.

During the earlier **Direct Examination**, I advised you to stand on the side of the jury box farthest from the witness stand in order to keep the jury's focus on your witness, rather than you.

Now, you need to come in close to the witness box. Not so close that you draw an objection, but at least to the podium that is usually placed about midway down the jury box. Stand just to the left of it so you are closer to the witness. You can have your notes on the podium. This is to get the jury's attention on you.

Cross Examination is about the lawyer, or the **Pro Se** party, conducting it. You want the jury listening to the questions you are asking, noticing the things *you* picked out as important. When you want the attention on the witness, you will be standing right next to her.

Further Entry into Evidence of Documents, Photographs and Tangible Items by Both Parties

Generally, this is done throughout the case, not at one specific time, and just as the Defendant is able to enter Evidence during your case during Cross Examination, you can introduce Evidence that you have authenticated later in the case. For instance, some jurisdictions may allow you to enter the deposition you used to impeach that witness as an exhibit although others only allow the testimony itself.

Presentation of Any Evidentiary Motions that Arise during the Case

Again, these are handled as they arise during questioning. You are ready with your research and your Memoranda of Law in your Trial Notebook.

Defendant Rests

Once the Defendant is satisfied that all the Evidence has been presented, the Defendant rests his or her case. This means the Defendant's case is finished and the matter cannot be thereafter reopened to introduce additional Evidence. It is now finished until Closing Argument.

Plaintiff Makes a Motion (Moves) for Directed Verdict

At this point, the Plaintiff can move for a Directed Verdict because the Defendant failed to meet the burden to prove the elements of the affirmative defenses or on the issue of negligence itself. The standard is just as stringent as for the motion when brought by the Defendant. This motion is less common, but can be just as important to preserve for Appeal if there is any genuine question.

Plaintiff May Bring Rebuttal Witnesses

Be very careful reserving witnesses for Rebuttal. I have seen lawyers who thought they were going to make their cases on Rebuttal, only to be denied the opportunity to bring in crucial witnesses. The standard is fairly steep.

84

When talking about **Rebuttal Witnesses**, "The proper function of rebuttal Evidence is to contradict, impeach or defuse the impact of the Evidence offered by an adverse party." Peals, 535 F.3d at 630 (quoting United States v Grintjes, 237 F.3d 876, 879 (7th Cir. 2001) (internal quotation marks omitted).[2]

In other words, you cannot use them to clarify your own case, but only to contradict, impeach or diffuse, like you would on Cross Examination. If your proposed Rebuttal Witnesses have valuable testimony, it is best to present it in your case rather than run the risk that it is not allowed at all.

Closing Arguments

Closing Argument is your time to shine. It is the time when you stand in front of the jury and "tell them what you told them."

Now you can say, "Remember in my Opening Statement when I told you that I was going to prove [X], [Y], & [Z]? Now you have heard from Mr. Neighbor, who told you [X], and the Expert, Mr. Remodel, who told you [Y]. You have seen photographs that show [Z] clearly. And what about Defendant who admitted [W] in her deposition, but tried to tell you [V] when called to testify here at the trial?" (Remember, you got in and out, quick like a snake.) "From all of this Evidence, it is clear that Defendant's negligence caused this fire and, therefore, I am entitled to $[___]."

You want to be as clear and concise as you can here as well, while still reviewing every piece of important Evidence. You want to talk about the critical parts of each witness's testimony as much as they are relevant to your case (and most, if not all, are).

You may also talk about the upcoming jury instructions in your Closing Arguments if there is something important you want to highlight. Start with the Instruction on your **Burden of Proof**. You want to explain to the jury how you have met it, so they understand what it is.

---

[2] *Rebuttal Witness Cannot Be Used To Clarify Evidence Offered in Case In Chief.* 12 Apr. 2008. Federal Evidence Review. 3 Sep. 2010. http://federalevidence.com/blog/2008/augu st/%E2%80%9Crebuttal%E2%80%9D-witness-cannot-be-used-clarify-evidence-offered-case-chief

In civil cases, the burden of proof is generally weighed by a **Preponderance of the Evidence**. You can explain to the jury that this does not mean the same thing as in criminal cases where the burden is "beyond a reasonable doubt."

Remind the jury it just means that you have a bit more convincing Evidence than the Defendant; just enough to tip a set of scales in your favor. Demonstrate this visually for them, by holding your hands level, palms upward, and then tipping them slightly. How much explaining you can do depends on your State and its laws.

One other thing to note is that you have a time limit for your argument. If you are the Plaintiff in this case, you also have the right to a **Rebuttal Argument** after the Defendant has given the Closing Argument. You must be sure to reserve sufficient time for this. It just depends on what you must cover in your primary argument and what you expect the Defendant to say.

Charges to the Jury

Jury Charges (Jury Instructions) are read to the jury, usually by the Court. They contain all the law that the jury can use to decide the case. These charges have either been agreed to or your objections to them have been heard at the Pretrial Conference.

The jury is not allowed to take copies of these instructions to the jury room with them; they must remember them as best they can. This is another reason for highlighting those charges important to your case.

Do pay attention during this phase. You want to show the jury how important it is. Listen intently. Not only does this show respect for the Court, but it is conceivable you could also catch an error that the Court might make which could harm your case. One word misspoken could change the entire meaning of a definition.

Avoid it if you can, but object if you need to. As with so many things, if you do not use it, you will probably lose it.

Jury Deliberations

The first thing they are instructed to do is choose a foreman who directs the deliberations and signs the jury form at the end.

A note about juries: every jurisdiction is different as to how and when you can approach the jurors. Everyone does agree, however, that you cannot approach a juror during the trial of the case. That means you do not even exchange pleasantries in the restroom. Now, Georgia has a rule that you can approach the jurors after the trial and after the verdict has been rendered, inquiring whether they would be willing to speak with you, then, if so, you can ask them about their verdict. This is a very helpful rule in that it allows you to get some valuable insight into how jurors really think and interact when they are back in the jury room. Florida, on the other hand, absolutely forbids any contact with jurors either during or after the trial. The thinking is that it chills the public's willingness to serve as jurors if they know they can be questioned afterwards.

After all the Arguments are finished and the Jury Instructions have been read, the jury is sent for Deliberations. It is important to keep eye contact with the jury while they are preparing to go, rather than shuffling your papers. This shows respect as well as a degree of confidence. Smile if you feel it is appropriate but avoid looking smug or arrogant. The jury is sent back with all the Evidence that has been entered in the case. That is all they have to look at, so you had better have made it good. What they do not have are the Jury Instructions and any Depositions that were read into Evidence because those are treated the same as any other witness.

The jury's first task is to elect a **Foreman** who directs the deliberations and signs the **Verdict Form**. After the Verdict, the losing party may be permitted to poll the Jury. This means that each juror has to individually state whether that was, in fact, his or her verdict.

Verdict

This is the moment you have been waiting for. You have spent a day or two, maybe more, trying your case and it all comes down to this. The Jury re-enters the courtroom and everyone stands. (Point in fact: you should always stand whenever the Jury comes in or goes out of the Courtroom. It shows respect.)

The Judge asks the Jury if they have reached a verdict. The **Foreman** answers yes. The Foreman then hands the **Verdict Form** to the **Bailiff**, who hands it to the Judge who reviews it and sends it back. The Foreman then reads the Verdict: "We, the Jury, find in favor of the Plaintiff in the amount of $[___]," or "We, the Jury, find in favor of the Defendant." The judge then thanks the Jurors for their time and dismisses them.

CHAPTER

7

IF YOU LOSE YOUR CASE

Motion for Judgment Notwithstanding the Verdict (JNOV)

At the time during the trial when a Jury furnishes its verdict, the losing party may move for a JNOV, a **Judgment Notwithstanding the Verdict** if they believe that no reasonable Jury could have found as this one did on the issue or issues in the original complaint. The Judge has the power to overturn the Jury's award and even modify a damages award. However, it is important to note that this is rarely done.

Appeal

If the Judge does not overturn the Jury's verdict, you may find yourself needing to **Appeal** a lower Court's decision. This means that you are asking a higher Court to review the outcome of the lower Court with the hope that the ruling may be overturned. (It is important to understand that Appeals Courts *do not generally review the facts of the case, but assume that the facts the lower Court deemed true are in fact true.*

The Appeals Court deals with the issues of law almost exclusively. Of course, there are exceptions to this rule, which are outside the scope of this book, but you should be aware just the same that having an Appeals Court review your case is not the same as having it retried on its merits.)

In Florida, the County Court, including a Small Claims Courts, appeal directly to the Circuit Courts. Circuit Court cases are appealable directly to the District Court of Appeal, which, in turn, takes its Appeals directly to the Supreme Court of Florida.

Cases from the Circuit Court can also be directly appealed to the Supreme Court of Florida, depending on the case. The District Court of Appeals can take Appeals from County Court cases where questions have been **certified** to that Court. The same is true, among other methods, for getting to the Supreme Court of Florida from the District Court of Appeal.

You may want to take some time early on to figure out the system in your home State, in case you find yourself needing to use it. You need to know how to maneuver from one Court to the other and determine how much it is going to cost.

Returning to your situation where you have just lose your case, you feel perhaps that the judge made some errors and you think you have a good chance of getting the case overturned on **Appeal**. What do you do? Remember that rulebook you bought? Chances are it has the Appellate Rules in it as well.

Most likely you have 30 days to file your Notice of Appeal in the lower Court. This tells the Clerk to bundle up a certified copy of the original Court File and send it to the Appeals Court. When you file your notice, you indicate what parts of the file you want sent. Note: you are paying for it and it is not cheap.

Again, make sure you know what Court you are appealing to. For instance, if you started in County Court in Florida, you would direct your Appeal to the Circuit Court, possibly even located in the same Courthouse as the County Court that heard your case.

EPILOGUE

By now you should be fairly familiar with the basic terminology of lawsuits. The glossary at the end of this book is a handy reference tool should you be unsure of any terms.

You should now also realize that winning your case is going to require considerable effort and research on your part. The trial process should no longer be a strange and alien landscape to you. You have a good grasp of the proceedings. You have been escorted through all the steps of the phases before and during the trial. You now know how to organize yourself. You are ready to go.

The trial experience, like anything else, is what you make of it. If you jump in with both feet, ready to work hard and learn everything you can, you can succeed. If you come into this halfheartedly, hoping that sheer luck will offset your unwillingness to invest time and effort on your own behalf, you will see a commensurate return on your investment. That said, even the most extreme effort is no guarantee that you are going to win your lawsuit. Even the most skilled lawyers lose occasionally. But it is fair to say that will not win unless you play to win. You must have the mindset and the work ethic to succeed.

After having read this book, you have what it takes to do just that. You know where to source the information you need beforehand to prepare and where to go for help if you need it. No book, class or even life experience as a trial lawyer can prepare someone for absolutely every possibility, but you have better odds on your side now. *Representing Yourself* will have given you the confidence it takes to successfully represent yourself in Court.

Good luck!

GLOSSARY

Affirmative Defenses: Defenses that the Defendant has which must be brought in the first responsive pleading or they are lost.

Alternates: Additional jurors who hear the trial but do not take part in deciding the verdict unless a juror is unable to deliberate.

Appeal: Seeking a higher Court to review and overturn the ruling of a lower Court.

Answer: The pleading filed by the Defendant(s) in response to the Complaint.

Bad Faith: In a civil case, not necessarily involving insurance, one can be found in bad faith if the case is brought merely for the sake of harassment.

Bailiff: Officer who keeps order in the Courtroom.

Bench Trial: Trial presided over and decided by the judge without a jury. Also called a Judge Trial.

Burden of Proof: In most civil matters the burden of proof is 'a preponderance of the Evidence'. This means simply a greater weight of the Evidence.

Caption: Sets forth the Court, the parties and the case number and will appear on the top of each pleading.

Case-in-chief: A party's primary case.

Cause of Action: The fact or facts that give Plaintiff the right to bring a claim against a Defendant.

Certified: A written attestation; an authorized declaration verifying that an instrument is a true and correct copy of the original.

Chain of Custody: The chronological documentation or paper trail, showing the seizure, custody, control, transfer, analysis, and disposition of evidence, physical or electronic, in order to avoid later allegations of tampering or misconduct which can compromise the case of the prosecution toward acquittal or to overturning a guilty verdict upon appeal.

Civil: Relating to private rights and remedies sought by civil actions, as contrasted with criminal proceedings.

Clerk's Office: Where all the original pleadings are filed and stored.

Closing Arguments: Final arguments made by a party to a jury regarding the case just tried.

Complaint: The pleading filed by the Plaintiff against one or more Defendants.

Compulsory Counterclaim: One that arises out of the same set of facts as the Complaint. Must be brought in the first responsive pleading or lost.

Counterclaim: Causes of action the Defendant has against the Plaintiff.

Court: A government body in which the administration of justice is delegated; sometimes used interchangeably with "Judge" during a bench (non-jury) trial.

Court Clerk: Person who keeps the judge's Court docket and helps move the trial along, marking exhibits, administering oaths, and so on.

Court Reporter: Makes a record of all the trial proceedings including depositions. Any or all can be transcribed for a party later, as in the case of Appeal.

Criminal: Relating to private rights and remedies sought by criminal actions as contrasted with civil proceedings.

Cross-claims: Claims multiple Defendants in a case have against each other.

Cross Examination: A party's questioning of his opponent's witnesses. Leading questions are generally allowed.

Declaratory Judgment: Asking the Court to pronounce that a specific position is the correct one.

Default: Failure to timely answer a lawsuit.

Default Judgment: A judgment entered against a party who fails to appear in court or respond to the charges.

Defendant: The person against whom a claim is brought in a lawsuit.

Demand Letter: A letter stating a legal claim, which makes a demand for restitution or performance of some obligation, owing to the recipients' alleged breach of contract, or for a legal wrong.

Demonstrative Evidence: Evidence in the form of a representation of an object.

Deposition: Testimony of a witness or a party taken under oath outside the courtroom, the transcript of which becomes a part of the court's file.

Direct Examination: A party's questioning of his own witnesses at the trial. Leading generally not allowed.

Discovery: The name given pretrial devices for obtaining facts and information about the case.

Documentary Evidence: Any evidence introduced at a trial in the form of documents, including any media by which information can be preserved, e.g., photographs, tape recordings; films and printed e-mails.

Equitable Jurisdiction: System of remedies based on fairness. See Injunction, Declaratory Judgment and Specific Performance.

Evidence: Testimony, documents, and tangible things presented to the jury in support of a party's position.

Expert Witnesses: Possess specialized knowledge, training or skill and are allowed to give opinion testimony.

Foreman: Person chosen by other jurors to direct deliberations and sign verdict.

General Denial: Denial of all allegations in a complaint; a denial that relates to all allegations not otherwise pleaded to.

Hearsay: An out-of-court statement offered to prove the truth of the matter asserted.

Impeach: To show a witness to be less believable; to bring the testimony into question.

Injunction: Asking the Court to stop someone from doing something.

Interrogatories: Written questions to another party that must be answered under oath.

Judge: A presiding officer of the court; also referred to as "Court" during a bench (non-jury) trial.

Judge Trial: A trial held before a judge sitting without a jury; also known as a bench trial.

Judicial Notice: Where the Court takes note of a fact or set of facts that are essentially common knowledge. The party is thereafter not required to prove them.

Jurors: A certain number of men and women selected according to law and sworn to try a question of fact or indict a person for public offense. Also referred to collectively as the Jury.

Jury Charges: Instructions to the jury on the law of the case being tried.

Law Clerk: Works for judges, helping them with their research and writing.

Lay Witnesses: Those without any specialized knowledge or skill, generally not allowed to give opinion testimony.

Leading Questions: A question that suggests its answer.

Memorandum of Law: A written legal document used in various legal adversarial systems that is presented to a court arguing why the party to the case should prevail; also referred to as a brief.

Motion: An application made to a court or judge that requests a ruling or order in favor of the applicant.

Motion for a Directed Verdict: Motion requesting that the court enter judgment in favor of the party filing the motion before submitting the case to the jury, because there is no legally sufficient evidentiary foundation on which a reasonable jury could find for the other party.

Motion for Continuance: Motion requesting the post-ponement of a hearing, trial, or other scheduled court proceeding at the request of either or both parties in the dispute, or by the judge, often when necessitated by unforeseeable events, or for other reasonable cause articulated by the person seeking the continuance, especially when the court deems it necessary and prudent in the "interest of justice."

Motion for Enlargement of Time: Motion requesting an extension of time during which a party may plead a case, file a requisite document in court, etc.

Motion for Judgment Notwithstanding the Verdict: A motion requesting that the court enter a judgment in favor of the party filing the motion, despite the jury's contrary verdict because there is no legally sufficient evidentiary basis for a jury to find for the other party. Under the Federal Rules of Civil Procedure, this procedure has been replaced by the provision for a motion for judgment as a matter of law, which must be presented before the case has been submitted to the jury but can be reasserted if it is denied and the jury returns an unfavorable verdict.

Motion for Protective Order: A party's request that the court protect it from potentially abusive action by the other party, usually relating to discovery, as when one party seeks discovery of the other party's trade secrets.

Motion for Summary Judgment: Motion requesting the court to decide that the available evidence, even if taken in the light most favorable to the non-moving party, supports a ruling in favor of the moving party.

Motion in Limine: Motion requesting that information which might be prejudicial not be allowed to be heard in a case.

Motion to Compel: Motion requesting the court to order either the opposing party or a third party to take some action; most commonly deals with discovery disputes, when a party believes that the discovery responses are insufficient.

Motion to Dismiss: Motion requesting the court to decide that a claim, even if true as stated, is not one for which the law offers a legal remedy.

Motion to Dismiss for Failure to State a Claim: Motion requesting that the court hold that the claim states no cause of action under the applicable substantive law.

Notice of Motion: Formal notification of the fact that a motion has been filed; also, any form of notification of a legal proceeding.

Offer of Settlement: Offer to settle for specific sum. If offer is refused, and conditions of offer are met, costs and sometimes fees will be taxed against party who declined offer.

Opening Statement: A party's opening remarks to the jury.

Order: A mandate, command, or direction given by a court or judge, made in writing.

Pain and Suffering: Measure of damages in a lawsuit.

Permissive Counterclaim: One that does not arise out of the same set of facts as the Complaint.

Plaintiff: Person who brings the lawsuit.

Pleading: Paper filed by a party to a suit containing claims or defenses.

Prayer for Relief: The portion of a complaint in which the plaintiff describes the remedies that the plaintiff seeks from the court.

Preponderance of the Evidence: Burden of proof in most civil cases. It means a greater weight of the Evidence.

Pretrial Conference: Conference between judge and lawyers to finalize matters for the trial.

Pretrial Memorandum: A written memorandum to the court setting forth each side's theory of the case, goals and justifications.

Pretrial Order: A court order setting out the rulings, stipulations, and other actions taken at a pretrial conference.

Prima Facie Case: A case that is sufficient and has the minimum amount of evidence necessary to allow it to continue in the judicial process.

Pro Se: Bringing or defending a legal action without a lawyer to represent you.

Real Evidence: Any material object, introduced in a trial, intended to prove a fact in issue based on its demonstrable physical characteristics; also referred to as material or physical evidence.

Reasonable Doubt: Any doubt that may exist in mind of a "reasonable person" that the defendant is guilty. There can still be a doubt, but only to the extent that it would not affect a reasonable person's belief regarding whether or not the defendant is guilty.

Rebuttal Argument: Occurs during the trial stage where evidence is given by one party to refute evidence introduced by the other party.

Rebuttal Evidence: Evidence given to explain, repel, counteract or disprove facts given in evidence by the opposing party; that which tends to explain or contradict or disprove evidence offered by the adverse party; evidence which is offered by a party after he has rested his case, and after the opponent has rested, in order to contradict the opponent's evidence. Also, evidence given in opposition to a presumption of fact or a *prima facie* case; in this sense, it may not be only counteracting evidence but evidence sufficient to counteract, that is, conclusive.

Rebuttal Witnesses: Used to contradict, impeach, or defuse the impact of Evidence offered by adverse party.

Redirect Examination: Opportunity to present rebuttal evidence after one's evidence has been subjected to cross-examination.

Request to Admit: A list of statements that one party is requesting the other to admit or deny.

Request to Produce: Written requests that one party produce documents and/or tangible items to another.

Return of Service: Sheriff returns with his signature and the day, date, and time of service on the Defendant.

Sidebar: Conference between the judge and lawyers next to the bench and outside the hearing of the jury.

Special Damages: Your past medical bills, future medical expenses, lost wages, lost earning capacity, and any expenses incurred to obtain medical care or while you are incapacitated, including child-care expenses.

Specific Performance: Asking the Court to require a person or entity to do a thing once promised.

Statute of Limitations: Time within which a cause of action must be brought.

Style of the Case: Sets forth the Court, the parties and the case number and will appear on the top of each pleading.

Strike a Jury: Where the parties choose a jury through a series of pre-emptory strikes.

Sue: To bring a lawsuit against a person or entity.

Summons: Tells the Defendant that he is being sued and a deadline for his Answer.

Testimonial Evidence: Evidence (excluding documents and physical evidence) that is given by a witness under oath.

Third Party Complaint: A petition filed by a defendant against a third party, not presently a party to the suit, which alleges that the third party is liable for all or part of the damages plaintiff may win from defendant.

Trial Brief: A written document prepared for and used at trial, containing the issues to be tried, synopsis of evidence to be presented and case and statutory authority to substantiate the attorney's position at trial.

Venue: Relates to a Court's ability to exercise jurisdiction over the person of the Defendant.

Verdict: The jury's decision on the case.

Verdict Form: A form filed delineating how the verdict should be formulated. A general verdict form requires the jury to apply the law to the facts and to find for either the plaintiff or the defendant;

special verdict forms require the jury to make written findings only on issues of fact.

Voir Dire: Initial questioning of prospective jurors before a jury is seated. Also refers to testing the qualifications of an opponent's expert.

LAW OFFICES OF
GARY M. ZEIDWIG, P.A.

ADVOCATE BUILDING, SUITE 200
315 SOUTHEAST 7TH STREET
FORT LAUDERDALE, FLORIDA 33301

TELEPHONE (954) 523-3993
FACSIMILE (954) 523-3665
WEBSITE: WWW.ZEIDWIGLAW.COM
E-MAIL: GZ@ZEIDWIGLAW.COM

May 12, 2011

State Farm Insurance Companies
Attn: Mr. Smith
State Farm Insurance Co.
P.O. Box 9618
Winter Haven, FL 33883-9618

Re:	Insured	:	XXXXXXXX
	Claimant	:	XXXXXXXX
	D/A	:	12/16/04
	Claim #	:	59-Y925-732

Dear Mr. Canada:

As you are aware our office represents XXXXXXX for the injuries sustained on December 16, 2004 on North S.R 7 (441) Coral Springs, FL. The injuries sustained by our client, XXXXXXX, were suffered as a direct result of your client's actions, as indicated on page 3 of the long form of the Florida Traffic Crash Report. Stemming from the accident our client has suffered injuries including:

1) Headaches
2) Injury to the cervical spine
3) Injury to the thoracic spine
4) Injury to the lumbar spine
5) Injury to the musculotendinous and ligamentous structures throughout the back and neck area
6) Myofascial I injury
7) Strain to the sacroiliac joints
8) Intermittent radiculopathy
9) Findings consistent with disk injury
10) Cervical disk herniations
11) Lumber disk injury
12) Loss of cervical and lumber lordosis
13) Lateral sided ligament injury to the right ankle

XXXXXXX sought medical attention in the time following the day of the accident. Her prognosis included treatment for all of the above listed injuries sustained from the collision where your client ran a red light and collided with our client. XXXXXX has undergone extensive treatment for the injuries sustained on North S.R. 7(441) Coral Springs, FL.

The following medical records have already been forwarded to your office for your review:

1) Dr. Ron Wechsel, Wechsel & Pain Rehab Center
2) Sandford Davis, Board Certified Radiologists
3) Mitchell R. Pollak, M.D., P.A. Board Certified Orthopaedic Surgeon & Board Certified Arthroscopic Surgeon

To assist you in your evaluation of XXXXXXXXX claim, the following is a summary of my client's medical bills:

MEDICAL PROVIDER	TOTAL	PAYMENT	BALANCE
Dr. Wechsel	$9,114.00	$6,976.43	$2,137.57
A-1 Open MRI	$3,700.00	$2,339.30	$1,360.70
Dr. Pollack	$1,360.56	$1,090.56	$270.00
TOTALS	$14,174.56	$10,406.29	$3,768.27

The serious injuries sustained by our client were caused solely by the negligence of your insured, XXXXXXX, in the operation of her vehicle. Your insured's liability is undisputed.

The final prognosis for XXXXXXX is that she sustained a whole person permanent impairment of four (4) to five (5) levels for the cervical spine showing loss of the cervical lordosis as well as herniations with multiple level disc injury, and four (4) to five (5) and five (5) to one (1) levels with loss of the lumber lordosis. In total, This incident occurring as a result of your client's/insured's actions has left XXXXXX impaired for life and for this reason we request compensation in the amount of $50,000.

Please respond to settle this claim within thirty (30) days from your receipt of this letter.

Very Truly Yours,

GARY M. ZEIDWIG
GMZ/rf

LAW OFFICES OF GARY M. ZEIDWIG, P.A.
ADVOCATE BUILDING, SUITE 302 · 315 S.E. 7TH STREET · FORT LAUDERDALE, FL 33301 · TELEPHONE (954) 523-3993

IN THE CIRCUIT COURT OF THE 17TH
JUDICIAL CIRCUIT IN AND FOR
BROWARD COUNTY, FLORIDA

CASE NO:
JUDGE:

Plaintiff,

vs.

Defendants,

_____/

COMPLAINT

COME NOW the Plaintiff, ▮▮▮▮▮ by and through their undersigned
attorney, and sues the Defendants, ▮▮▮▮▮▮▮▮▮ and ▮
▮▮▮ and alleges that it is entitled to relief on the following facts:

GENERAL ALLEGATIONS

1. This is an action for damages in excess of Fifteen Thousand ($15,000.00)
Dollars, exclusive of interest, costs and attorney's fees.

2. This Court has jurisdiction over this action pursuant The Florida Rules of
Civil Procedure.

3. Venue is proper in Broward County, Florida because all parties to this
action reside in Broward County, Florida, and it is also where the causes of action sued
upon herein occurred.

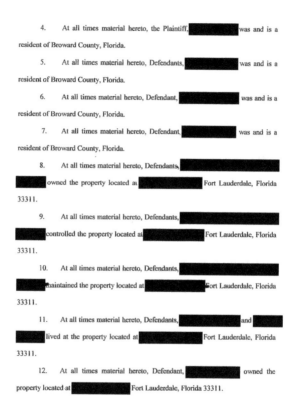

4.   At all times material hereto, the Plaintiff, ▮▮▮▮▮▮ was and is a resident of Broward County, Florida.

5.   At all times material hereto, Defendants, ▮▮▮▮▮▮ was and is a resident of Broward County, Florida.

6.   At all times material hereto, Defendant, ▮▮▮▮▮▮ was and is a resident of Broward County, Florida.

7.   At all times material hereto, Defendant, ▮▮▮▮▮▮ was and is a resident of Broward County, Florida.

8.   At all times material hereto, Defendants, ▮▮▮▮▮▮ ▮▮▮▮ owned the property located at ▮▮▮▮▮▮ Fort Lauderdale, Florida 33311.

9.   At all times material hereto, Defendants, ▮▮▮▮▮▮ ▮▮▮▮ controlled the property located at ▮▮▮▮▮▮ Fort Lauderdale, Florida 33311.

10.   At all times material hereto, Defendants, ▮▮▮▮▮▮ ▮▮▮▮ maintained the property located at ▮▮▮▮▮▮ Fort Lauderdale, Florida 33311.

11.   At all times material hereto, Defendants, ▮▮▮▮▮▮ and ▮▮▮▮ lived at the property located at ▮▮▮▮▮▮ Fort Lauderdale, Florida 33311.

12.   At all times material hereto, Defendant, ▮▮▮▮▮▮ owned the property located at ▮▮▮▮▮▮ Fort Lauderdale, Florida 33311.

106

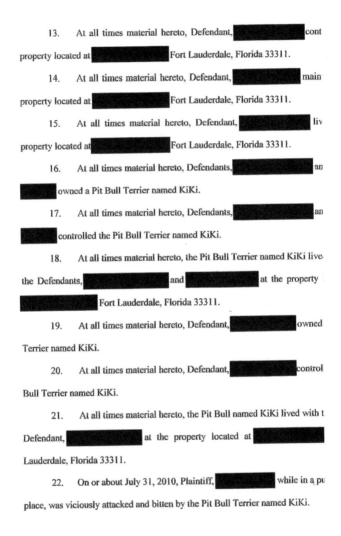

13. At all times material hereto, Defendant, ██████████ cont

property located at ██████████ Fort Lauderdale, Florida 33311.

14. At all times material hereto, Defendant, ██████████ main

property located at ██████████ Fort Lauderdale, Florida 33311.

15. At all times material hereto, Defendant, ██████████ liv

property located at ██████████ Fort Lauderdale, Florida 33311.

16. At all times material hereto, Defendants, ██████████ an

██████████ owned a Pit Bull Terrier named KiKi.

17. At all times material hereto, Defendants, ██████████ an

██████████ controlled the Pit Bull Terrier named KiKi.

18. At all times material hereto, the Pit Bull Terrier named KiKi live

the Defendants, ██████████ and ██████████ at the property

██████████ Fort Lauderdale, Florida 33311.

19. At all times material hereto, Defendant, ██████████ owned

Terrier named KiKi.

20. At all times material hereto, Defendant, ██████████ control

Bull Terrier named KiKi.

21. At all times material hereto, the Pit Bull named KiKi lived with t

Defendant, ██████████ at the property located at ██████████

Lauderdale, Florida 33311.

22. On or about July 31, 2010, Plaintiff, ██████████ while in a pu

place, was viciously attacked and bitten by the Pit Bull Terrier named KiKi.

107

23.   The unprovoked vicious attack by the Pit Bull Terrier named KiKi was a complete surprise to the Plaintiff, ███████████.

24.   The Pit Bull Terrier named KiKi was picked up and placed into quarantine as the dog had not previously been administered the vaccinations which are required in the State of Florida.

25.   As a result of the above-described dog bites, ███████████ suffered severe and permanent injuries and scarring.

COUNT I
STRICT LIABILITY UNDER §767.04 Fla. Stat
(As to Defendants, ███████████ and ███████)

Plaintiff, ███████████ re-alleges paragraphs 1 thru 4, 6 thru 11, 16 thru 18 and 21 thru 25 as if fully set forth herein and would further state:

26.   Under §767.04, Fla. Stat., Defendants, ███████████ and ██████ are liable for damages caused by their dog's bites, to Plaintiff, ███████████.

27.   At all times material hereto, Plaintiff, ███████████ was lawfully in a public place when bitten by Defendants' dog.

28.   As a direct and proximate result of being bitten, Plaintiff, ███████████ was injured in and about his body and/or aggravated a pre-existing condition or injury, suffered pain there from incurred medical and related expenses in the treatment of his injuries, suffered physical handicap, suffered psychological and emotional injuries, sustained permanent injuries with a reasonable degree of medical probability and/or permanent loss of bodily function and has lost the capacity for the enjoyment of life.

29.   In that the injuries suffered by the Plaintiff, ███████████ are continuing in nature, plaintiff will continue to suffer pain, psychological and emotional injuries, loss

of wages, physical handicap and permanent injury in the future and will be further compelled to expend great sums for medical care and related treatment for those injuries.

WHEREFORE, Plaintiff ███████ demands judgment for damages against the defendants, ███████ and ███████ together with costs and demands trial by jury of all issues triable as of right by jury.

COUNT II – NEGLIGENCE
(As to Defendants, ███████ and ███████

Plaintiff, ███████ re-alleges paragraphs 1 thru 25 as if fully set forth herein and would further state:

30.   Defendants, ███████ and ███████ owed a duty to the Plaintiff, ███████ to protect him from attacks by dogs on their property.

31.   Defendants, ███████ and ███████ knew or should have known that the Pit Bull Terrier named KiKi lived with the Defendant, ███████ on their property located at ███████ Fort Lauderdale, Florida 33311.

32.   Defendants, ███████ and ███████ knew or should have known that allowing the Pit Bull Terrier named KiKi lived with the Defendant, ███████ on their property located at ███████ Fort Lauderdale, Florida 33311 would posed a danger to others and in fact caused the plaintiff to be bitten.

33.   Defendants, ███████ and ███████ did not take the necessary pre-cautions to prevent the dog bites sustained by the Plaintiff, ███████

34.   As a proximate result of the dog bites, the Plaintiff, ███████ suffered severe injuries, pain and suffering.

35.   As a direct and proximate result of the negligence of the Defendants, ███████████ and ████████████, Plaintiff, ████████████ was injured in and about his body and/or aggravated a pre-existing condition or injury, suffered pain there from incurred medical and related expenses in the treatment of his injuries, suffered physical handicap, suffered psychological and emotional injuries, sustained permanent injuries with a reasonable degree of medical probability and/or permanent loss of bodily function and has lost the capacity for the enjoyment of life.

36.   In that the injuries suffered by the Plaintiff, ████████████ are continuing in nature, plaintiff will continue to suffer pain, psychological and emotional injuries, loss of wages, physical handicap and permanent injury in the future and will be further compelled to expend great sums for medical care and related treatment for those injuries.

WHEREFORE, Plaintiff ████████ demands judgment for damages against the defendants, ████████████ and ████████████ together with costs and demands trial by jury of all issues triable as of right by jury.

COUNT III
STRICT LIABILITY UNDER §767.04 Fla. Stat
(As to Defendants, Sheen N. Morris)

Plaintiff, ███████ re-alleges paragraphs 1 thru 5, 12 thru 15 and 19 thru 25 as if fully set forth herein and would further state:

37.   Under §767.04, Fla. Stat., Defendant, ███████ are liable for damages caused by their dog's bites, to Plaintiff, ███████

38.   At all times material hereto, Plaintiff, ███████ was lawfully in a public place when bitten by Defendant's dog.

39.   As a direct and proximate result of being bitten, Plaintiff, ███████ ███████ was injured in and about his body and/or aggravated a pre-existing condition or injury, suffered pain there from incurred medical and related expenses in the treatment of his injuries, suffered physical handicap, suffered psychological and emotional injuries, sustained permanent injuries with a reasonable degree of medical probability and/or permanent loss of bodily function and has lost the capacity for the enjoyment of life.

40.   In that the injuries suffered by the Plaintiff, ███████ are continuing in nature, plaintiff will continue to suffer pain, psychological and emotional injuries, loss of wages, physical handicap and permanent injury in the future and will be further compelled to expend great sums for medical care and related treatment for those injuries.

WHEREFORE, Plaintiff ███████ demands judgment for damages against the defendants, ███████ and ███████ together with costs and demands trial by jury of all issues triable as of right by jury.

COUNT IV – NEGLIGENCE
(As to Defendant, ███████████**)**

Plaintiff, ███████████ re-alleges paragraphs 1 thru 5, 12 thru 15 and 19 thru 25 as if fully set forth herein and would further state:

41. Defendant, ███████████ owed a duty to the Plaintiff, ███████████ to protect him from attacks by her dogs.

42. Defendant, ███████████ knew or should have known that allowing the Pit Bull Terrier named "KiKi" to lived with her at the property located at ███NW ███ Court, Fort Lauderdale, Florida 33311 would posed a danger to others and in fact caused the plaintiff to be bitten.

43. Defendant, ███████████ did not take the necessary pre-cautions to prevent the dog bites sustained by the Plaintiff, ███████████

44. As a proximate result of the dog bites, the Plaintiff, ███████████ suffered severe injuries, pain and suffering.

45. As a direct and proximate result of the negligence of the Defendant, ███████████ Plaintiff, ███████████ was injured in and about his body and/or aggravated a pre-existing condition or injury, suffered pain there from incurred medical and related expenses in the treatment of his injuries, suffered physical handicap, suffered psychological and emotional injuries, sustained permanent injuries with a reasonable degree of medical probability and/or permanent loss of bodily function and has lost the capacity for the enjoyment of life.

46. In that the injuries suffered by the Plaintiff, ███████████ are continuing in nature, plaintiff will continue to suffer pain, psychological and emotional injuries, loss of wages, physical handicap and permanent injury in the future and will be

further compelled to expend great sums for medical care and related treatment for those injuries.

WHEREFORE, Plaintiff ███████ demands judgment for damages against the Defendant, ███████ together with costs and demands trial by jury of all issues triable as of right by jury.

Respectfully Submitted,

GARY M. ZEIDWIG, P.A.
Attorney for Defendant
315 Southeast Seventh St., Suite 302
Fort Lauderdale, Florida 33301
Telephone: (954) 523-3993
Fascimile: (954) 523-3665

By:_____
GARY M. ZEIDWIG, ESQ.
FLORIDA BAR NO: 0418498

IN THE CIRCUIT COURT OF THE 15TH
JUDICIAL CIRCUIT IN AND FOR
PALM BEACH COUNTY, FLORIDA

CASE ███████████████████

JUDGE: ███████████

███████████

    Plaintiff,

Vs.

███████████

    Defendants.

_____/

PLAINTIFF'S MOTION FOR LEAVE TO AMEND COMPLAINT TO ADD CLAIM FOR PUNITIVE DAMAGES AGAINST DEFENDANTS AND SUPPORTING MEMORANDUM OF LAW

    Plaintiff, ███████████ by and through undersigned counsel, and pursuant to Florida Statute 768.72 and Florida Rule of Civil Procedure 1.190(f), hereby move this court for leave to amend the complaint to add a claim for punitive damages against Defendant, ███████ and in support thereof, states as follows:

I. Background

    This is an action for damages which includes significant personal injuries to the Plaintiff, ███████████ sustained as a result of the accident caused by the negligent driving of Defendant, ███████████ On April 6, 2010, Defendant, ███████████ operated a 2009 blue Lincoln Continental automobile in a southbound direction on *U.S. 441* in a negligent manner, so as to cause Defendant's automobile to collide into the rear end of the 2001 Mercedes Benz automobile being operated by

Plaintiff, ███████████ The Defendant was negligent in so that he attempted to drive the rented automobile while under the influence of several different chemical substances which were later identified as Suboxone and Klonopin. Upon investigating the accident, the officers observed the Defendant, ███████████ g asleep at the wheel. Furthermore when he was questioned by officers, he was slow to respond and had poor motor skills. The Defendant, ███████████ was then given a field sobriety test and was unable to complete three of the five proffered task. He later consented to a urine test for chemical substances. The Defendant, ███████████ subsequently pled guilty to driving under the influence.

II. Legal Argument

A. ˸   Leave To Amend Should Be Freely Granted

Florida Rule of Civil Procedure 1.190(a) provides that leave of court to amend a pleading "shall be given freely when justice so requires." *Id.; see also Dimick v. Ray*, 774 So.2d 830, 833 (Fla. 4th DCA 2000). The decision whether to allow the amendment of a pleading is within the trial court's discretion. *See Yun Enters., Ltd. v. Graziani*, 840 So.2d 420, 422 (Fla. 5th DCA 2003). "However, the trial court's discretion should be exercised in accordance with the public policy of this state to freely allow amendments so that cases may be resolved on their merits." *Mass v. State*, 927 So.2d 157, 161 (Fla. 3d DCA 2006); *Torrey v. Leesburg Regional Medical Center*, 769 So.2d 1040, 1044 (Fla. 2000). "Courts should be especially liberal when leave to amend is sought at or before a hearing on a motion for summary judgment." *Bill Williams Air Conditioning & Heating, Inc. v. Haymarket Coop. Bank*, 592 So.2d 302, 305 (Fla. 1st DCA 1991) (quotations omitted).

"As a general rule, leave to amend should not be denied unless the privilege has been abused, there is prejudice to the opposing party, or amendment would be futile." *N. Am. Speciality Ins. Co. v. Bergeron Land Dev., Inc.*, 745 So.2d 359, 362 (Fla. 4th DCA 1999) (quotations omitted); *see also Video Independent Medical Examination, Inc. v. City of Weston*, 792 So.2d 680, 681 (Fla. 4th DCA 2001)

("Refusal to allow amendment constitutes an abuse of discretion unless it clearly appears that allowing the amendment would prejudice the opposing party, the privilege to amend has been abused, or amendment would be futile.")

None of the aforementioned grounds apply to the instant facts and, thus there is no applicable basis to deny Plaintiffs' motion for leave to amend the amended complaint. Plaintiffs have properly sought leave only after first engaging in discovery which identified the appropriate grounds upon which to state a claim for pleading punitive damages. *See Life General Sec. Ins. Co. v. Horal*, 667 So.2d 967, 969 (Fla. 4th DCA 1996).

B.   *The Legal Standard For A Motion For Leave To Amend To Add A Claim For Punitive Damages Is Quite Low*

To plead a claim for punitive damages, a plaintiff must first "obtain leave from the trial court to amend the complaint". *Stephanos v. Paine*, 727 So.2d 1075, 1076 (Fla. 4th DCA 1999); *see Simeon, Inc. v. Cox*, 671 So.2d 158, 160 (Fla. 1996). Once leave is sought, a plaintiff must then comply with § 768.72, Florida Statute which require an initial "showing by evidence in the record or proffered by the claimant which would provide a reasonable basis for recovery of such damages." § 768.72(1), Fla. Stat.; *see Simeon, Inc.*, 671 So.2d at 159.

Indeed, while the evidentiary standard required for proving punitive damages at trial is quite high, the pleading standard for amending a complaint to add a claim for punitive damages is quite low. *Compare* § 768.725, Fla. Stat. (requiring clear and convincing evidence) with § 768.72(1), Fla. Stat. (requiring only a reasonable showing). Essentially, the Florida courts inquiry into the merits of a motion to amend to add a claim for punitive damages is analogous to the standard applied in determining whether a complaint states a cause of action. *See Holmes v. Bridgestone/Firestone, Inc.*, 891 So.2d 1188, 1191 (Fla. 4th DCA 2005) ("When a trial court is determining if a plaintiff has made a reasonable showing under section 768.72 for a recovery of punitive damages, it is similar to determining whether a complaint states a cause of action . . . .") Thus, a "reasonable basis" exists where there is "evidence tending to show that punitive damages could be properly inflicted." *Doral Country Club, Inc. v. Lindgren Plumbing Co., Inc.*, 175 So. 2d 570, 571 (Fla. 3d DCA 1965). "If an award of punitive damages may be supported under any view of the evidence taking all inferences most favorable to the plaintiff, a jury issue is made and whether to award such damages is rightly decided by the jury . . . ." *Johns-Manville Sales Corp. v. Janssens*, 463 So. 2d 244, 248 (Fla. 1st DCA 1984) (emphasis added). Within the framework of this standard, Plaintiffs record evidence and/or proffer must be viewed as true in the light most favorable to them. *See Wallace v. Dean*, 3 So.3d 1035, 1043 (Fla. 2009).

Applying the relevant legal standards set forth above, the evidence proffered herein undoubtedly provides a reasonable basis for recovery of Plaintiffs punitive damages claim and, thus, exceeds the especially low threshold necessary to add such a claim to the instant complaint.

C.   *The Defendant's Guilty Plea to DUI is a "Reasonable Basis" To Add A Claim For Punitive Damages*

Recognizing the low threshold necessary to plead a claim for punitive damage, it is clear that a "reasonable basis" evidencing Defendants egregious, wanton and reckless behavior exists and supports Plaintiffs motion for leave. It came to be argued that intoxicated driving cases, by their very nature, ought to be categorically within the jury's authority to award punitive damages. In *Ingram v. Pettit*, 340 So.2d 922 (Fla.1976), the court confronted the issue "whether a jury should be allowed to consider an award of punitive damages where negligence is coupled with intoxication." *Id.* at 923. The court went on to state "we hold that juries may award punitive damages where voluntary intoxication is involved in an automotive accident in Florida without regard to external proof of carelessness or abnormal driving, provided always the traditional elements for punitive liability are proved, including proximate causation and an underlying award of compensatory damages. We do not hold that intoxication coupled with negligence will always justify an award of punitive damages. We affirmatively hold that the voluntary act of driving 'while intoxicated' evinces, without more, a sufficiently reckless attitude for a jury to be asked to provide an award of punitive damages if it determines liability exists for compensatory damages."; in such context, term "while intoxicated" means same as it does in criminal proceedings and is not synonymous with "under the influence of intoxicating liquor." *Id.* at 923. Significantly, the record reveals that Defendant, ████████ pled guilty to driving under the influence and has a certified conviction from January 10th 2011.

As a result, the evidence proffered herein supports Plaintiffs' Motion and this court should enter an Order grant same.

D. *There Is No Requirement Or Need For An Evidentiary Hearing To Grant Plaintiff Motion*

In discussing the requirements of section 768.72(1), the court in *State of Wisconsin Investment Board v. Plantation Square Associates, Ltd.,* 761 F.Supp. 1569 (S.D. Fla. 1991), made it patently clear that "a proffer according to traditional notions of the term, connotes merely an offer of evidence and neither the term standing alone nor the statute itself calls for an adjudication of the underlying veracity of that which is submitted, much less for countervailing evidentiary submissions." *Id.* at 1581 n. 21 (quotations omitted). Indeed, as shown *supra,* a reasonable proffer at this stage must take the form of depositions testimony, answers to interrogatories, and requests for admissions. The court is required only to make a sufficiency determination that such a proffer meets the requirements of § 768.72(1), Fla. Stat. and does not test the veracity of the record evidence presented. *See Henn v. Sandler,* 589 So.2d 1334, 1335-36 (Fla. 4th DCA 1991) (Only "the legal sufficiency of the punitive damage pleading is in issue in the section 768.72 setting."). As a result, an evidentiary hearing on a motion for leave to add a claim for punitive damages is neither contemplated nor mandated by the statute in order to determine whether a reasonable basis has been established. *See Solis v. Calvo,* 689 So.2d 366, 369 n. 2 (Fla. 3d DCA 1997) ("Pursuant to Florida Statute section 768.72, a punitive damage claim can be supported by a proffer of evidence. A formal evidentiary hearing is not mandated by the statute.") (citation omitted)

119

(emphasis added); *Strasser v. Yalamanchi,* 677 So.2d 22, 23 (Fla. 4th DCA 1996) ("[A]n evidentiary hearing is not mandated by the statute before a trial court has authority to permit an amendment. Pursuant to section 768.72(1), a proffer of evidence can support a trial court's determination."). Accordingly, any request for hearing on this Motion is unwarranted and contrary to Florida's statutory and decisional law.

CERTIFICATE OF SERVICE

I HEREBY CERTIFY that a true and correct copy of the foregoing has been furnished to ███████

██████████████ located at ████████████████████████ Florida

███ this 25th day of May, 2011.

Respectfully submitted,

GARY M. ZEIDWIG, P.A.
Advocate Building, Suite 302
315 Southeast 7th Street
Fort Lauderdale, FL 33301
Telephone: (954) 523-3993
Facsimile: (954) 523-3665

BY:_____
GARY M. ZEIDWIG, ESQ.
Florida Bar No.: 0418498

IN THE CIRCUIT COURT OF THE 17TH
JUDICIAL CIRCUIT IN AND FOR THE
COUNTY OF BROWARD, FLORIDA

CASE NO:

████████

Plaintiff,

Vs.

████████ Inc.,

Defendant.

_____ /

**PLAINTIFF'S REQUEST FOR ADMISSIONS
TO DEFENDANT,** ████████

TO: DEFENDANT, ██ Department Stores, INC.
By **Service of Summons upon its Registered Agent.**

████████

BRADENTON, FL. 34208

Pursuant to the provisions of Rules of Civil Procedure 1.370, you are hereby requested and required to respond to the following Request for Admissions consisting of ten (10) Requests within forty-five days from the date of service of Summons to the Office of GARY M. ZEIDWIG, P.A., 315 Southeast Seventh Street, Suite 200, Fort Lauderdale, Florida, 33301:

1.   Admit or deny that you owned, operated, maintained and/or controlled the indoor premises for the ▆▆▆ Department Store. located at ▆▆▆▆▆▆▆▆▆▆ Fort Lauderdale, FL. 33308, Broward County, Florida on December 14, 2004.

2.   Admit or deny that Plaintiff was injured inside the ▆▆▆ Department Stores, INC. located at ▆▆▆▆▆▆▆▆ Fort Lauderdale, FL. 33308, Broward County, Florida on December 14, 2004.

3.   Admit or deny that Plaintiff was injured inside the ▆▆▆ Department Stores, located at ▆▆▆▆▆▆▆▆ Fort Lauderdale, FL. 33308, Broward County, Florida on December 14, 2004, due to the negligence of your employee, servant, and/or agent.

4.   Admit or deny that at the time and location where Plaintiff was injured inside the ▆▆▆ Department Store, located at ▆▆▆▆▆▆▆▆ Fort Lauderdale, FL 33308, Broward County, Florida on December 14, 2004, there was no wet floor sign out.

5.   Admit or deny that the substance was on the floor for a period of time before the subject incident.

6.   Admit or deny that the Defendant, its agents, employees, or representatives were aware of the substance on the floor prior to Plaintiff's fall.

7.   Admit or deny that Plaintiff slipped on a wet floor inside the ▮▮▮▮ Department Store, located at ▮▮▮▮▮▮▮▮▮▮ Fort Lauderdale, FL. 33308, Broward County, Florida on December 14, 2004.

8.   Admit or deny that the failure to put out a wet floor sign or other type of warning to people inside the ▮▮▮ Department Stores, located at ▮▮▮▮▮▮▮▮ Fort Lauderdale, FL. 33308, Broward County, Florida on December 14, 2004, just prior to Plaintiff's slipping and falling was negligent.

9.   Admit or deny that on December 14, 2004, there should have been a wet floor sign to warn of the hazard.

10.   Admit or deny that on December 14, 2004, the Plaintiff was not warned of the hazard.

11.   Admit or deny that on December 14, 2004, the Plaintiff slipped and fell inside the ▮▮▮ Department Store, located at ▮▮▮▮▮▮▮▮▮ Fort Lauderdale, FL. 33308, Broward County, Florida because of the hazardous wet floor.

12.   Admit or deny that an incident report was filled out regarding the subject
accident by Defendant herein.

13.   Admit or deny that the accident on December 14, 2004, was reported and
noted that the wet floor was the cause of the Plaintiff's fall.

14.   Admit or deny that at the time of the incident Plaintiff, ██████████
was a business invitee.

    WE HEREBY CERTIFY that a true and correct copy of the foregoing Request for
Admissions will be served by Summons upon the Defendant ██████ Department Stores,
INC., this _____ day of _____ 200__.

                                GARY M. ZEIDWIG, P.A.
                                Attorney for Plaintiff
                                315 SE Seventh Street
                                Suite 200
                                Fort Lauderdale, FL 33301
                                (954) 523-3993
                                (954) 523-3665 - Fax

                                BY:_____
                                    GARY M. ZEIDWIG
                                    Fla. Bar No.: 0418498

ACKNOWLEDGMENTS

My deepest thanks to my parents, Carol and Howard Zeidwig, who have been my never-ending support and confidants, my sister, Melissa, for reminding me to always do the right thing, my brother, Eric, for his loyalty and friendship, and my coach, publisher, and above all, friend, Sheila Danzig, for her ongoing encouragement and brilliant ideas. I would also like to express my thanks to my clients, past, present, and future, for their trust and support.

ABOUT THE AUTHOR

Gary Zeidwig hails from southern Florida and obtained his JD from Florida's Nova University Law School after graduating from the University of Florida. Zeidwig is a member of the Federal Bar and is licensed to practice law in the US District Court in Florida's Southern District. Before starting his own private practice, Zeidwig spent three years with the Public Defender's office in Broward County, Florida. For well over a decade, Zeidwig has represented clients in court, in both bench and jury trials.

Zeidwig bases his practice in Fort Lauderdale, Florida, and provides all prospective clients with a free initial consultation. If you have inquiries or would like to make an appointment, telephone Zeidwig at (954) 523-3993.